# THE PRIVATE LIFE
### of the
# EMPRESS JOSEPHINE

# THE PRIVATE LIFE

of the

# EMPRESS JOSEPHINE

by

CHARLES KUNSTLER

*Adapted from the French by Herma Briffault*

DAVID McKAY COMPANY, INC.

New York

MANUFACTURED IN THE UNITED STATES OF AMERICA

VAN REES PRESS • NEW YORK

# Contents

PART III. *Josephine, Empress of the French*
(1804-1809)

PART IV. *The Empress in Retirement*
(1809-1814)

# Foreword

A YEAR before the marriage of his eldest daughter, Monsieur Tascher de la Pagerie wrote to the prospective groom's father, the Marquis de Beauharnais, describing her. "She has a very fine complexion, beautiful eyes, beautiful arms, and a surprising aptitude for music," he declared, adding, "I saw to it that she had instruction in playing the guitar during the time she was in convent school; she turned the lessons to good account, for she has a lovely voice."

What happened to these physical charms when depicted by the brushes and the pens of those painters and compilers of memoirs who were on familiar terms with the Empress Josephine?

At the Louvre you will see two portraits of her, one by Prud'hon, the other by David. Prud'hon lets us see her in the leafy shades of Malmaison, a red shawl flung over a white dress flecked with gold sequins. Her head is slightly inclined; her coffee-brown eyes, gentle and glowing, soften still more the tender expression of her features. Her milky-white shoulders, arms, and bosom are more striking than her face. Her hair is parted in the middle, its chestnut-brown hue intensified by golden bands encircling her forehead. In the other painting, the "Coronation of Napoleon," begun by David in 1805 and finished in 1808, Josephine's complexion is not so luminous, and her hair is of a darker chestnut, almost mahogany brown.

In the Empress's bedroom at Malmaison hangs a portrait bust of her by Gérard. The jewels of her crown sparkle above dark-brown hair; her face is carefully made up; her brown eyes look at you with a poignant curiosity. Even next to her white robe and the ermine which touches one of her shoulders, her delicate, rosy-white flesh has the sheen of ivory.

The great artist Delacroix pronounced in favor of the portrait by Prud'hon, saying that he had managed, in addition to capturing an exquisite pose, to achieve a perfect resemblance. This "resemblance" permits us to judge how much trust we can place in the biographers of the Empress Josephine.

If we are to believe Lucien Bonaparte, his sister-in-law had "very little wit, nothing of what might be called beauty, but a hint of her Creole blood in the supple movements of her body which was smaller than average. Her face was without natural freshness, although it is true the resources of the dressing table rendered it effective enough by lamplight."

Napoleon's valet, Constant, described the Empress Josephine as being of medium height and "in pleasure as well as suffering, beautiful to behold. Her dark-blue eyes were almost always half-hidden beneath heavy eyelids. Her hair was long and silky, and its light-chestnut color admirably suited the tone of her dazzlingly fresh and fine complexion."

Madame de Rémusat, a lady in waiting, affirmed for her part that, "without being precisely pretty, Josephine's entire person possessed a peculiar charm. There was delicacy and harmony in her features. The expression of her eyes was gentle; her mouth, which was very small, concealed bad teeth. The slightly dark hue of her skin could not be detected beneath the powder and rouge that she cleverly applied. Her figure was perfect, her limbs were lithe and finely formed.... She possessed a rather exquisite and natural tact, readily finding agreeable things to say...."

Throughout the nineteenth century and into our own, his-

torians have delighted in listing Josephine's charms. I have
dipped into some of these books and found a wealth of con-
tradictory evidence: sometimes Josephine's hair is blond, sometimes brown; her eyes are sometimes dark blue, sometimes
light brown. This is only to be expected, since these descriptions are based on the memories of intimates of the Empress,
who are in disagreement about her beauty or lack of it.

If the accuracy of these writers must be doubted when they
portray her physically, according to their personal tastes and
prejudices, how can we believe them when they presume to
portray her morals? To the disfigured portrait painted by
Lucien Bonaparte in his bitter *Mémoires* the ambitious in-
grate, Madame de Rémusat, added her own further dis-
tortions. And the volatile and verbose Duchesse d'Abrantès
ascribed a great many thoughts, words, and acts to the Empress
which documentary evidence often refutes. Corrupt and cynical men, such as Barras and Bourrienne, avenged themselves
upon the Master by circulating deceitful anecdotes about
everyone close to him.

To justify Josephine, some writers have felt obliged to turn
the Emperor into a kind of domestic tyrant. To glorify Napoleon, others have felt obliged to debase his first wife. Going
back into her past, they have turned doubtful or enigmatic
documents to their advantage in confirming their preconceived
and often unfavorable opinions. Thus, the sudden voyage of
the Vicomtesse de Beauharnais to Martinique in 1788, which
can be so easily explained, some writers have tried to turn into
a shameful flight designed to conceal an illicit pregnancy.
Other writers, in depicting Josephine at the Carmelite Prison,
have made her the mistress of General Hoche. Her relations
with Paul de Barras have been described in profuse detail—and
what detail! And the scene in which Bonaparte pardoned
her upon his return from Egypt has often been ridiculously
romanticized.

It took a writer as impartial and well armed with facts as

Jean Hanoteau to destroy these legends. The numerous and precise notes with which he has enriched his various books on the subject throw a new light on the private life of Josephine.

A spiteful rival disrupted her first marriage. The second one was broken up by the avowed hatred of the Bonaparte family for the Beauharnais, a hatred as inexpiable as that of the Montagus and Capulets, and one which was quelled neither by the divorce of Josephine and Napoleon nor by the separation of Louis Bonaparte—that insanely jealous Romeo—and Hortense de Beauharnais, a loveless Juliet.

Like her father, Gaspard Tascher de la Pagerie, Josephine knew nothing of certain middle-class virtues. She was not a heroine; but she knew how to be pleasing and lovable. She charms us still, with her courteous manners, her gentle grace, her sweetness—the seductiveness of Racine's heroines. Napoleon said it eloquently to Queen Hortense, not long after Waterloo: "I never saw anyone so filled with grace. She was woman in the fullest sense of the word: mercurial, vivacious, and with the kindest of hearts ..."

# Part I

## ROSE, THE VICOMTESSE DE BEAUHARNAIS

### (1763-1796)

# 1

## *Rose of the Isles*

ON THE western coast of Martinique, at the foot of hills which dominate Fort Bourbon, is the port of Fort-de-France, known as Fort-Royal before the French Revolution. The ramp of the fortress, which several times defended the colony from English attack, is now used as a promenade, sheltered from the tropical sun by tamarind trees and from the trade winds by the surrounding hills and mountains. Across the bay, to the southeast, may be seen three rocky islets from which the little town on the adjacent shore takes its name: Trois-Ilets. Here, on June 23, 1763, Marie Josèphe Rose Tascher de la Pagerie was born, who was destined to become Josephine, Empress of the French.

Both her parents were of good Creole, French colonial, stock, and two grandparents were on hand to act as godparents at her christening: her maternal grandfather, Joseph des Vergers de Sanois, and her paternal grandmother, Marie Françoise Tascher de la Pagerie. It was in honor of her mother, Rose Claire, that she received the name Rose by which she was known during the first thirty years of her life, until she met young General Bonaparte, who chose to call her Josephine. It is by the name Rose that we must learn to think of her through the years of her first unhappy marriage, during which, despite some acquired sophistication, she remained to a great

3

extent the charming Creole girl who was born and grew up in Martinique.

Little is known of her mother except that the Vergers de Sanois were a very old titled family, originally from the province of Brie; and that her maternal grandfather died in 1767, leaving enormous debts.

More is known of Rose's father, Gaspard Tascher de la Pagerie—son of a titled Orléans family—who was sent to France as a boy to act as page in the household of the King's daughter-in-law, the Dauphine Marie Josèphe; and he retained throughout his life dazzling memories of the court at Versailles. He returned to Martinique in 1755, shortly before the outbreak of the Seven Years' War, as a second lieutenant in the colonial navy. During the war he was lieutenant of the coast gunners and distinguished himself during the bombardment of Fort-Royal by the English fleet. By the time the Treaty of Paris was signed in 1762, and Martinique was returned to France, Gaspard had been honorably discharged from the army with a pension of 450 livres and had retired to Trois-Ilets with his bride to become a sugar planter.

Improvident and indolent, his health undermined by a recurring tropical fever and occasional debaucheries in Fort-Royal, Gaspard paid scant attention to business matters, so that they were already in a bad way when the great hurricane of 1767 practically destroyed the hamlet of Trois-Ilets and his plantations. By that time his wife had borne him two more daughters—Catherine Désirée and Marie Françoise—and his father-in-law had died, leaving only debts. Thus, when Rose was only four years old, her father was already worrying about supporting his family and trying to find husbands who would support his daughters in the future.

After the hurricane, Gaspard moved his family into the sugar refinery, which, being built of stone, had withstood the catastrophe. Gradually, the slaves' cabins were rebuilt, but for years there could be no thought of rebuilding the family house.

Someone must be found to help, and Gaspard thought about his remarkable sister Désirée, who lived in Paris, separated from her husband, Alexis Renaudin. She had once been a noted beauty in Martinique, and had proved herself very resourceful.

During the war, when the Marquis de Beauharnais had for a time been royal governor of Martinique, the vivacious blond beauty of Désirée Tascher de la Pagerie had been very attractive to him. His wife, the marquise, had noticed it and discovered, she thought, a way to remove the coquette from her husband's life: she found a husband for Désirée—Alexis Renaudin, one of the marquis's orderlies and a noted roué. Unfortunately for the marquise, the marriage did not last long. Before a year had passed, Désirée returned to her family, and made no objection when Monsieur Renaudin went to Paris and filed suit for a separation. Désirée was still in Fort-Royal on June 10, 1760, when she acted as godmother to the second son of the Marquis de Beauharnais. This son—about whose parentage there seems to have been some gossip—was Alexandre de Beauharnais, who was destined to become the husband of Rose, as yet unborn. Shortly after this christening, Désirée de Renaudin returned to France. A year later, the Marquis and Marquise de Beauharnais also returned to France, leaving the child Alexandre with Désirée's mother at Fort-Royal, giving as a reason that he was too young for the long voyage.

At the age of five, Alexandre was sent to France, but in the meantime the Marquis and Marquise de Beauharnais had separated and she had retired to her estate in Blois. The marquis was living with Madame Renaudin at her house on the Rue Garancière in Paris. Despite everything, Désirée had won her distinguished lover; and when the marquise died, not long after Alexandre's arrival in France, Désirée's beloved godchild came to live with her and the marquis. During that period, which was so much influenced by the writings of Jean Jacques Rousseau, an irregular household such as that on the Rue Garancière caused almost no lifting of eyebrows.

The little "chevalier," as Désirée referred to Alexandre in her letters to Gaspard de la Pagerie, was placed in a boarding school, along with his elder brother François, whom Désirée was also mothering. Since one of the duties of a French mother was to arrange betrothals for children scarcely out of their cradles, Madame Renaudin was very soon discussing the subject in her letters to her brother. Generous hearted, she could not forget, in her relative prosperity, her impoverished brother and his family in Martinique. Marriages must be arranged, not only for her godsons but for her nieces. As the years wore on, her letters were filled with urgent pleas that at least the eldest girl, Rose, be sent to France, where Désirée could supervise her education and perhaps arrange a suitable marriage.

When Gaspard showed these letters to his wife the question always arose: Where would they find the money for the voyage? Their income was barely sufficient for their daily bread. And so the years passed.

But for Rose they were happy years. As a young child she was allowed to run wild around the plantation until she was ten. From her black nurse, Marion, she learned the songs of the region; and from romping and playing in the gardens that surrounded the house, she learned to love flowers. Music and flowers were to be her lifelong joys, and in the letters written in later life to her son, there are wistful references to the flowers of the tropical island—the acacia, jasmine, heliotrope, orange blossoms, and her own flower, the rose. From her childhood years she retained a fear of the wind, which seems to have begun with the night of the great hurricane. When the warning bell sounded, the entire household—master, mistress, and slaves—rushed out of the house for greater safety and stood watching the boats, houses, and fields smashed and laid waste by the gigantic waves that swept the shore. Rose's nurse Marion snatched her from her cradle and held her in her arms.

Madame de la Pagerie held her second daughter, Catherine Désirée. It was twenty days after the hurricane that the third child, Marie Françoise, was born.

Rose watched the slaves at work, and sometimes, on feast days, she danced and sang with them. In the orchards there were dwarf lemon trees, "mombin" plums, and "cinnamon apples," and when Rose was not eating their fruit she was sucking sugar cane. Sometimes she would climb the low hill to the church where she had been baptized; then, running down toward the sea, she would pause before a Madonna set in a stone niche and, after a moment of contemplation, wander along a path which lost itself in the hills. There were deep gorges down which mountain torrents rushed and tumbled in the rainy season. It was a wild land, and a wild but pleasant life.

When she was approaching her tenth birthday, Rose was sent to board with the nuns of the Dames of the Providence at Fort-Royal. Actually, little was taught there except prayers, singing, and embroidery, but life became regulated. Early mass was at seven o'clock, and classes began at eight after another prayer, when the girls knelt and chanted *Veni Creator Spiritus*. The luncheon break was from eleven to one o'clock. Afternoon classes ended at five, when the girls were taken on a regimented walk. On Saturday and Sunday, Rose usually spent the afternoons with her grandmother, Madame de la Pagerie, who lived with her Aunt Rosette. Gaspard's elder brother, the Baron Tascher, dropped in sometimes. The baron was a gay and lively uncle who liked to recount his numerous adventures. During a naval battle against the English, a saber had slashed his skull, and after the war he had been appointed captain of the port. It was largely because of him that Fort-Royal became a well-enough equipped harbor to accommodate a large fleet.

It was the Baron Tascher who brought Rose to her ballet master, Monsieur Francis, for her weekly lessons in dancing and "deportment." Afterward he would take her for a stroll, sometimes to a hilltop where the inhabitants of the town often gathered to admire the sunset.

At vacation time, Rose returned home to Trois-Ilets, where her life was again one of indolence and innocent pleasures. She often recalled, in later years, long, lazy afternoons in a hammock, lying with eyes half-closed, listening to the sound of the sea and dreaming of mysterious and faraway France, to which she was being summoned ever more urgently by her Aunt Désirée's letters.

The routine of boarding school ended for Rose when she was fifteen. That year her younger sister, Catherine Désirée, died, and Rose grieved deeply over her first bereavement. Gaspard Tascher de la Pagerie now had only two daughters for whom to find husbands, but time was pressing. Rose, at fifteen, had much womanly charm. Her features were still softened by the glow of youth, but her fair hair had turned light auburn, her beautiful arms and bosom were no longer those of a child —nor was the look in her eyes. Her clear, captivating voice was acquiring a deeper and more vibrant note. Rose was becoming a woman.

The letters exchanged by Gaspard with his sister in Paris became more explicit and practical. The elder son of the marquis, François, had recently married his cousin, the eldest daughter of Fanny de Beauharnais, the poetess. This made Désirée all the more anxious to arrange a betrothal between her godchild Alexandre and one of her nieces in Martinique. She wrote that such a marriage would clear up Alexandre's "uncertain position in relation to the marquis"—and said she had already consulted Alexandre on his preference. The young man, then eighteen, preferred someone less near his own age than Rose, and it had been more or less agreed that Alexandre should marry Gaspard's second daughter, who was also a godchild of Madame Renaudin. The Marquis de Beauharnais left the matter in Madame Renaudin's hands and was "not particular" about a dowry.

The death of Catherine Désirée upset these plans, and in the same letter in which he announced her death, Gaspard offered his third daughter, Marie Françoise (called Manette), who was at the time only eleven and a half years old. But, he added, Rose had now left the convent, and he was a little worried lest she be upset over a betrothal of her younger sister. "Were it only up to me," he wrote, "I would bring you both of them"—meaning that Désirée could then choose between them.

"Come with one or both of your daughters," wrote Madame Renaudin in reply. She felt her godson Alexandre deserved "perfect happiness" and left it to Gaspard to decide which of his daughters had the necessary qualities. The Marquis de Beauharnais himself wrote, urging Gaspard to leave Martinique without delay and to bring the daughter he thought "best suited" to his son. The marquis enclosed in his letter a power of attorney which would allow Gaspard to have the banns published. On this document, the first name of the prospective bride was left blank.

At this point Gaspard was suddenly deprived of the right to choose the bride. All the women in his family, including his mother-in-law, Madame de Sanois, suddenly joined in strong protest against the preference he showed for his younger daughter.

In any case, it is clear that Rose herself had little if any choice in the matter, and we can only imagine what her thoughts must have been when, one summer day in the year 1779, she embarked on the cargo boat *Isle-de-France* for the long and dangerous journey across the Atlantic. Accompanying her were her father, her Aunt Rosette, and a mulatto maid, Euphémie, who happened to be the daughter of her old nurse Marion. The vessel was convoyed by the battleship *Pomone*, for British warships were everywhere on the high seas. The revolt of the American colonies had already produced several naval encounters.

It was a rainy day in early autumn when the *Isle-de-France* dropped anchor in the harbor of Brest, after a stormy passage. The town, under a gray sky, looked gloomy and sad, and there was no one to meet the weary voyagers. When they reached their lodgings in the Saint-Louis quarter, Gaspard fell ill and had to go to bed. Rose remembered all her life that the skies were dark and the rain was falling when she first set foot on the soil of France.

# 2

## *The Vicomte Takes a Wife*

A FEW DAYS later, the prospective bride and groom confronted each other in the presence of their elders, who watched the Vicomte Alexandre de Beauharnais with particular anxiety. What would his verdict be? Both he and his godmother, Madame Renaudin, had come down to Brest posthaste, as soon as word had reached them of the ship's arrival from Martinique. Alexandre had recently been promoted captain in the Sarre infantry regiment under the command of the Duc de la Rochefoucauld, and looked very handsome indeed in his new white broadcloth uniform with silver-gray lapels and cuffs. Rose could not conceal her admiration. How charming he was! And how nice! She was fascinated by the young officer, whose looks and manners strongly attracted her. Madame Renaudin's eyes went from her niece to her godson, speculatively. Rose was well "developed" for her sixteen years; she did not look much younger than the nineteen-year-old Alexandre. Her bearing was gracious, despite her provincial clothes. Her arms were beautiful, and her hands and feet were small and well shaped. And, though her face was calm and composed, her eyes under long thick lashes seemed to flash an ardent message.

Alexandre remained noncommittal, and Madame Renaudin spent some anxious hours on the journey back to Paris. They made the trip by easy stages in the first week of November, and it was with infinite relief that Désirée watched Rose's sweetness and gentle manners gradually break down Alexandre's resistance. On November 6, she triumphantly wrote to the marquis from Rennes that things were "going better and better," and Alexandre added a few words of his own: "The pleasure of Mademoiselle de la Pagerie's company," he declared to his father, "has been the only reason for my silence." He referred to Rose as "the girl to whom the name of your daughter sounds so sweet."

Madame Renaudin's anxiety had been well founded. Alexandre had admitted having an affair with a married woman, with whom he was desperately in love. He had disclosed this when she had broached the subject of his possible marriage to one of her nieces. Alexandre's mistress was one of his cousins, Laure de Girardin, wife of Monsieur de la Touche de Longpré, a naval officer in Brest. He had even used the word "despair" to describe his feelings at the thought of being torn from her, and Madame Renaudin was well aware that Laure de la Touche, eleven years older than Alexandre, was a dangerous rival for the innocent young Rose. Laure had the advantages of her age and social position, her worldly ways. Rose had the promise of youth and novelty, and life in Paris would improve her. With good advice, she could be "trained," Madame Renaudin kept telling herself, and would win Alexandre from Laure.

The wedding took place at one of Madame Renaudin's houses in Noisy-le-Grand, near Paris, and was attended by some thirty guests, among them Alexandre's former tutor, Patricol, a professor of mathematics and a notorious pedant. Monsieur de la Pagerie, who had been taken ill again, could not be present and was represented at the ceremony by a relative, the Abbé Tascher, prior of Sainte-Gauburge.

The Vicomte Alexandre de Beauharnais's property had

been inherited from his mother and grandmother, it was sufficient to provide a comfortable income. The marriage contract
stated that Marie Josèphe Rose Tascher de la Pagerie contrib-
uted a dowry of 120,000 livres, "an advance" on her future
inheritance. Of this amount, her father kept back 20,000
francs to pay for her trousseau. The balance was to be paid in
installments every six months. Madame Renaudin gave her
niece the house at Noisy with all its furnishings, reserving for
herself the right to make occasional use of it.

The young couple set up housekeeping in Paris, in a house
belonging to the groom's father, the Marquis de Beauharnais.
Rose enjoyed some happy months at that house on the Rue
Thévenot, where she was surrounded with unaccustomed com-
forts and luxuries in which she took naïve delight. She never
tired of exclaiming over the jewels Alexandre had given her,
and sometimes on walks with her aunt she would take jewels
along simply for the pleasure of handling them. Her eagerness
and naïveté amused and charmed both Madame Renaudin
and the Marquis de Beauharnais.

But her amiable ways were not enough for her exacting
young husband, who refused to take her out in society. He
found fault with her education and drew up a course of study
for her, promising that when she had completed it he would
take her out with him. Her modesty and docility, the gay, sensitive, fresh spirit that had so enchanted him for a while began to pall. He was soon agreeing with his friends, who had
marveled at his attachment to an ignorant little Creole. To
them she seemed self-conscious, clumsy, without manners, and
not even very pretty. They had wondered particularly when
Laure de la Touche's husband died, and Alexandre still remained at home with his young wife.

It was not long before Alexandre became less attentive and
started going out alone. He was openly ashamed of the girl he
had married. Though naturally submissive and gentle, Rose
sometimes complained, and when she questioned him about

his absences, there were harsh words, tears, and sulking on both sides. Alexandre could be very ironical, even scornful and cynical, and to end these scenes which he considered beneath him he would boast of his successes in society, his good looks, his talent as a dancer, his wit.

Rose had to accept his terms. And while Alexandre danced and played in theatricals at the Duc de la Rochefoucauld's and other great houses of France, she stayed at home with her aunt and father-in-law who were crushed at the collapse of all their hopes and plans.

Alexandre was a great admirer of the popular philosophers, especially Jean Jacques Rousseau whom he idolized, and he wanted to turn Rose into a bluestocking who would star in fashionable *salons*. She must educate herself by reading more and more books, as he willed. What a difference between Rousseau's Sophie and the seventeen-year-old Rose, who wanted only to love and be loved! Alexandre argued the importance of literature, history, science; she retorted that life was worth more than all books.

But in the first year of their marriage Rose became pregnant, and there was an added excuse to confine her to the house on the Rue Thévenot. After the novelty of luxury had worn off, it had become to her a dark, airless kind of prison where there was little to see from any window, and only a tiny garden separating it from the street. Throughout her pregnancy, she could only continue her studies obediently while Alexandre went from party to party, from château to château.

That year, after he had returned to his regiment, he wrote her several rather affectionate letters, but they also contained moral dissertations to enlighten her. He sometimes referred to the unborn child with some tenderness. But the distance between them soon increased the discord, and Rose's unhappiness became so apparent that Madame Renaudin wrote to Alexandre's former tutor, Professor Patricol, asking him to use his influence with the irresponsible young man.

Madame Renaudin's letter reached Patricol when he and Alexandre were both guests of the Duc de la Rochefoucauld at Roche-Guyon. The old pedant, in a long and ponderous reply, quoted Alexandre's own harsh words:

"When I first met Mademoiselle de la Pagerie," the vicomte had declared, "I thought I could be happy with her, and immediately drew up a plan for her re-education. My project was wrecked by Rose's unwillingness, indifference, and negligence. Instead of staying at home with a woman who has nothing to say, I have gone back to my bachelor's life." Alexandre then referred to his wife's jealousy, which was undoubtedly justified: "Instead of turning to books and the development of her mind, my wife became jealous of me. She wants my life to be entirely devoted to her, wants to know what I say, do, and write; and never thinks of acquiring the real means of attaining this end by gaining that confidence which I regretfully withhold but which I shall grant her at the first sign she gives of wanting to be better instructed and pleasanter in behavior."

Alexandre returned to Paris in September, 1781, to be present at the baptism of his son Eugène. For a time, the birth of the child seemed to bring about a reconciliation of the parents, but Alexandre was soon off again, sowing his wild oats.

Rose had plodded through a long history of Rome by the Abbé Vertot, read a number of volumes by the "good poets," had learned whole plays by heart, and even consulted some atlases to please her exacting husband. All to no avail! Two months after the birth of Eugène, Alexandre left for Italy.

Rose's father and Aunt Rosette were with her in France until the birth of the child, but now they returned to Martinique and Rose's only companions were her Aunt Désirée and the Marquis de Beauharnais. Fortunately, Madame Renaudin was utterly devoted to her, and that summer she accompanied Rose to the house in Noisy.

For a few brief weeks Rose thought she had won Alexandre's love. Now, bewildered by his coldness, she began to question herself and to seek advice from Madame Renaudin. What was wrong? Had she not obeyed him and given him every loving attention he could desire? When he reappeared a few months later, he could see with his own eyes that during her second pregnancy she did not interrupt the course of reading he and Professor Patricol had drawn up for her.

In one quarrel, Alexandre asserted that only a Paris shop-keeper could be satisfied with the idle existence that she expected him to share with her. A military man, he said, could not endure this stagnant life. He was already twenty-three years old and had attained only the rank of captain. He was ambitious, and world events seemed to be playing into his hands. The revolt of the American colonies continued, and British warships were cruising in the region of Martinique where there had been one naval encounter between the French and the English. Alexandre wanted a post that would take him into the danger zone and thus lead to promotion. Fortunately for him, the Marquis de Bouillé, governor of the Windward Islands, was then in France, preparing to leave for Martinique. Putting his faith in the support of the Duc de la Roche-foucauld, Alexandre applied to the Marquis de Bouillé for the post of aide-de-camp.

His application was ignored, and the Marquis de Bouillé departed shortly afterward. Rose was delighted: her husband would stay with her. But his failure exasperated Alexandre. He was not wanted as an aide-de-camp? Then he would go to Martinique simply as a volunteer! He made his plans accordingly.

In thirty-three months of marriage Alexandre had spent at the most ten months with Rose, who was now in the fourth month of her second pregnancy.

Apparently weary of arguing with his wife and his god-mother, and wanting to avoid a parting scene, the vicomte left in the dead of night, without saying good-by to anyone. The marquis was astounded, Madame Renaudin was indignant, and Rose was crushed. From Brest, however, where he was waiting to embark, Alexandre wrote to reassure her—but maintained absolute silence as to his plans. His first letters contained many passages of tenderness, assurances of affection both for his wife and little son. He found charming words for the unborn child as well, the child that would be born during his fathers' absence in a distant land. He believed and hoped it would be a boy, and asked that it be given a name illustrious in Roman history: Scipio.

These letters from Alexandre, written from Brest in the early autumn of 1782, reveal the many facets of his character: impulsive, fickle, inconstant, secretive, given to extremes in both tenderness and anger. After a letter full of tenderness there would follow one full of reproaches. He complained particularly that Rose's letters were not as frequent or as lengthy as he had expected and wished. Did she no longer love him? This pregnancy was turning out to be a difficult one, and he became anxious about her health, giving her many admonitions to take good care of herself and "little Scipio." The tender letters always ended with declarations of undying love: "O my beloved, think of the child you are carrying, take care of him and of yourself. Look after Eugène, take good care of him. Think often of your husband, for he loves you and will love you all his life. Good-by, my sweetheart, good-by."

The following letter could not have been more churlish, reproachful, and self-pitying: "Another mail has come," he wrote, "and no news from you. Obviously I was right to leave. I would also be right to try to forget you. Among the departing men, I saw men happier than I, men whose wives were more loving, who wept at the departure of their husbands, told them they would be missed. While I, who perhaps deserve more than they, am forsaken. Well, if you cannot send a letter to Paris on courier days, although you have two lackeys, I shall have to write to others for news of you and your son. Farewell, Madame. You will cause me much anxiety during my voyage, but I shall try to make glory compensate for the pains of love."

The mail from Rose, which had been delayed, arrived while he was sealing this letter, but it failed to appease his wrath.

"You never had any love in your heart," he wrote the next day. "I shall do my best to follow your example. If our marriage is a failure, you have only yourself to blame. My intentions are good, my feelings most tender. But I shall embark with my judgments, my regrets, and my resolution.... May they forever, instead of ruining my health, dispose my heart to happy indifference. Good-by!"

His stay in Brest, however, was prolonged enough for him to write still more letters. In one he asked her forgiveness for any grief his "nasty letters" had caused her, but a new storm broke on October 21, when he wrote again complaining of her silence and of her irritation at his complaints: "You say harsh things to me when I dare complain of your silence. Is it my fault if your letters don't reach me? Do you prefer to have me indifferent to your neglect rather than to feel hurt at an apparent wrong inflicted upon me?" This letter, which he thought would be his last, ends on a gloomily romantic note: "It may be that the grief which overwhelms me will prove a boon. In the hazards of war and on the high seas, where I go to seek death, I shall welcome it with neither sorrow nor regret. Let death deprive me of a life in which every moment was marked by unhappiness. Farewell!"

Far from reassuring her, this, and the following letter, awakened and rekindled Rose's jealousy. The Vicomte Alexandre de Beauharnais informed his godmother that Laure de la Touche, his former mistress, had arrived in Brest. She had recently suffered a bereavement: her father had died and she was going to Martinique to settle her inheritance. Brazenly, he had asked Madame Renaudin to send a gift to Laure, a lotto game!

On November 18, Alexandre finally embarked on a ship named the *Venus*. And on the 26, from the Basque Roadstead, he wrote what was to be almost his last letter of love to his young wife. In it he implored her to remember him, saying, "I love you. And to my prayer that you will always think of me, I join a thousand kisses and a pledge of affection which shall end only with my life."

The twenty-three-year-old husband had a short memory, for on December 19, from the island of Aix, where contrary winds were holding up his vessel, he again wrote in anger: "I was hoping to receive a letter from you, but my hopes proved vain. Once, when I was at La Rochelle, you wrote to me, out of kindness. I suppose it was hoping too much that you would renew this pleasure. Is it possible that a wife can refuse to comfort a poor husband who seems destined to be tossed from coast to coast without ever reaching his destination?" He asked her to excuse the letter because he was "wild with rage," but before the apology he implied that Rose was capable of being unfaithful to him during his long absence.

It was a preposterous accusation, considering his own, open infidelity. On December 21, when favorable winds allowed the *Venus* to steer a course into open sea, the vessel carried not only Rose's husband but also Madame Laure de la Touche.

# 3

## *The Separation*

IMMEDIATELY upon his arrival in Martinique, the Vicomte de Beauharnais reported to the governor, Monsieur de Bouillé, who was certainly not expecting him and who informed him that the preliminaries of peace had been signed with England. Hostilities had ceased between Britain and her American colonies, now known as the United States, and long-standing quarrels between England and France, England and Spain, over boundaries and island possessions, were being settled by the treaty makers in Paris. It was good news for the world, but bad news for the ambitious young Alexandre, whose hopes of advancement were now ruined.

After paying a visit to the Baron and Baroness Tascher, he went to Trois-Ilets to see his wife's family. His visit was a surprise, but he was warmly welcomed. They exclaimed over a recent portrait of Rose he had brought them, and the women of the household, none of whom had seen Rose's handsome young husband, devoured him with their eyes. Manette found him utterly charming and could not understand how her sister could find any fault in him. Why did Rose complain in her letters? The expression in Alexandre's eyes was so gentle! And how elegant and witty he was! She only wished she had a husband like him. Grandmother de Sanois was also captivated.

Only Monsieur de la Pagerie had some reservations about

the impulsive, touchy, and temperamental young officer, but he showed Alexandre over the plantations and made him acquainted with the setting in which Rose had spent her girlhood. In a few hours the Vicomte de Beauharnais knew all the personal problems, illnesses, and prospects of her family. Monsieur de la Pagerie's health was still bad, preventing him from closely superintending the plantations and the refinery. The recurrent winds had recently destroyed his crops and obliged him to go into debt. Manette, pretty as she was, suffered from scurvy, the disease that was eventually to take her life.

From Trois-Ilets Alexandre wrote Rose an affectionate letter with all the family news, and so full of tenderness that her hopes were raised anew. He declared that he was eager to return to France, to see her again and hold her in his arms; only her love could compensate for the loss of a glorious military career.

Rose almost let herself forgive his whims and tantrums; but more and more the memory of his cruelty oppressed her and became intolerable. She knew too well how changeable he was, how easily influenced, to doubt that a violent mood would follow this period of calm. She could not forget her financial embarrassments, the despair in which he had left her, with a small child and about to give birth to another.... Much better to tear out from her heart the intense feeling he had inspired in her; she would not answer his letter; she would not write to him any more.

Rose was now living with her father-in-law and aunt in a house situated on the Rue Charles in the Faubourg Saint-Honoré. Her life in this new house was still gray and monotonous. To escape it, she sometimes spent afternoons at the Convent of the Dames of the Visitation, where aristocratic women lived in retirement from society. Among them was Alexandre's aunt by marriage, the Comtesse Claude de Beauharnais, known to the world of literature as Fanny, the poetess. Fanny had been a woman of great worldliness, and she was very much attracted to her nephew's young wife. She marveled at Rose's fidelity to a husband who had abandoned her and did not even have the grace to conceal his own infidelities. When Rose gave birth, in April, 1783, to her second child, Fanny hurried to her side and volunteered to act as godmother to the baby girl, who was christened Hortense.

At that time, Rose had an annual allowance of only 3,600 livres. In order to pay for her daughter's baptism, she had to sell a gold medallion that had been given to her by her father-in-law.

Meanwhile, in Martinique, Alexandre left Trois-Ilets after only a day and a half. He preferred Fort-Royal, where Laure de la Touche was staying. He lived almost openly with her, but for the Baron and Baronesse Tascher he allowed himself to be feted and flattered by the prettiest women in the city. He flirted with them all, but always returned to Laure de la Touche.

At the news of the birth of his daughter, Alexandre rejoiced, until Laure poisoned his happiness by a few questions and pointed remarks. Too bad, she said; he had wanted a Scipio, and had been given only a Hortense. She then asked for details and dates. Alexandre laughingly declared he had performed his conjugal duties the very night of his arrival in Paris from Italy, July 25, 1782. Laure commented, with a thoughtful air: "So, Hortense was born on April 10, that is to say, two hundred and fifty-nine days later—which makes eight months and sixteen days . . ."

The next day Laure attacked even more directly. In the midst of a reception, when Alexandre was being congratulated on the birth of his daughter, and was expressing his intention of returning to France, Laure stopped him with a gesture. How could he believe the child was his? The guests exchanged astonished glances, and then all eyes were turned upon Laure and Alexandre. "Didn't you tell me," she was asking him, "that your wife's pregnancy lasted two hundred and fifty-nine days? That means a dozen days short of the necessary nine months."

The suspicions which had tormented Alexandre for so long had suddenly been put into words. Rose had betrayed him. That explained her silences when they were apart and the indifference for which he had so often reproached her. But when had it begun? How long had she been deceiving him? He wanted to know everything about her, to look into her past and find out the secrets of her life as a girl in Martinique.

From that disastrous afternoon reception he went directly to the house of Aunt Rosette, who had accompanied Rose to France and lived with them in the house on the Rue Thévenot for more than two years. She would know.

Aunt Rosette, a homely and gossipy old maid, was not surprised or outraged by Alexandre's questions. In Paris she had seen and heard nothing. But in Martinique . . . ah, yes, there had been certain long-standing rumors. Before leaving the island, Rose had given cause for much talk. Oh, doubtless, her acts had been merely those of a thoughtless hoyden. . . . All the same, there had been that affair with a regimental officer stationed in Martinique, a Lieutenant Beaulieu or Berthelot. Rosette was not quite sure of the name, but if Alexandre made close inquiries he would soon learn the truth.

The ladies of Fort-Royal were only too ready to confirm the vicomte's suspicions. A Madame du Turon was particularly obliging and declared she had often met Mademoiselle de la Pagerie in the streets or seen her under the tamarind trees— and not always alone. An affair with an officer? Why, of course! And that affair had soon been followed by another, with a Monsieur d'Heureux. As a woman to whom such things were not new, Madame du Turon was able to name exact hours and places of rendezvous. According to her, Brigitte, a colored servant, had been given her freedom, in exchange for her silence on Rose's affairs. Louis, another slave who had recently died, had carried the notes exchanged by the lovers. Moreover, even during preparations for her voyage to France, Mademoiselle de la Pagerie had taken advantage of her grandmother's and mother's siestas to receive her lover in her bedroom! Her father was away and she had fooled the whole family, Madame du Turon declared.

The details were precise, but Alexandre could not believe in so much deception on Rose's part. How could he learn what truth there was in all this? Nothing could be easier, Laure assured him. He could loosen the tongues of the slaves at Trois-Ilets with gold, and she herself would help him question those who had been in Rose's service.

At first, Brigitte appeared not to understand Laure's questions, but when Alexandre pressed her, she declared that everyone at Trois-Ilets had loved the young mistress. True, her presence at Fort-Royal or at Trois-Ilets seemed to attract a number of army or naval officers. But that was a natural thing for any charming young girl. Brigitte maintained she had never seen Rose alone with any of the officers anywhere. Her father, mother, or uncle had always accompanied her. Letters? She had never received any. People were falsely accusing her former mistress. "I bear witness before God," said Brigitte.

Alexandre tried to trick her. "Your mistress told me," he said, "that she had written once to Monsieur d'Heureux and had received several letters from him. She said you were entrusted to put these letters away in a box to hide them from Madame de la Pagerie. She charged me, her husband, to ask you for them. Go fetch them. I will give you ten gold pieces for each one of them."

He took out the coins and jingled them before her eyes. "Come, don't be afraid, you have nothing to fear. It was your mistress who told me to ask you for them."

But Brigitte steadfastly maintained her own and Rose's innocence. "You can imprison me or torture me," she said. "I cannot say anything else."

Another slave, Maximin, lacked the courage to refuse Alexandre's money and told him everything the strange husband seemed to want to know. The news soon spread that the Vicomte de Beauharnais was handing out gold to "buy his wife's dishonor" and an eager crowd soon gathered. The stories they told were so exaggerated and farfetched that Eugène became "the son of several officers" of the regiment stationed in Martinique. Some of the talebearers even offered to show Alexandre the room in which the child had been born. A Creole of Fort-Royal presented Alexandre with a child allegedly born to Mademoiselle de la Pagerie before she had left for France, even though the child was only two years old and four years had passed since Rose's departure.

Alexandre was so disturbed by this unexpected abundance of lies and contradictions that he could not bring himself to write the letter to his wife that Laure had hoped he would. There was a delay, a period during which his mistress gradually worked up his fury. The letter he finally wrote to Rose was delirious with anger and jealousy, full of outrageous threats. Laure was on the point of returning to France and offered to deliver the letter directly into Rose's hands.

When she had embarked, Alexandre took out his rage on his godmother, Madame Renaudin. How could she have made him marry a girl whose reputation was so compromised? The Baronesse Tascher, to whom he also expressed his grief and anger, tried to quiet him, but in vain. She reproached him for having fallen under the influence of Madame de la Touche, an intriguing and perverse woman who was bent upon destroying his marriage. Alexandre persisted in his laments and accusations, blaming Rose's mother and grandmother, criticizing the upbringing Rose had had in Martinique . . .

Soon after this, Alexandre fell ill and being no longer welcome at the home of the Taschers he accepted the hospitality of Monsieur du Turon. There was a rumor that the young vicomte so misused this hospitality that Monsieur du Turon locked up his wife one night and the next day turned Alexandre out.

Rebuffed on every side, Alexandre finally decided to return to France. Still shaking with fever, he embarked on the *Atlante*, August 18, 1783, after a violent argument with his father-in-law. Monsieur de la Pagerie wrote him a bitter letter: "So this is the result of your voyage and your hopes for a fine campaign against the enemies of the State. Instead, you have made war on your wife's reputation and on the tranquillity of her family."

At the house in the Faubourg Saint-Honoré, spring had passed in anxious waiting. Alexandre had written in April, in May, then in June, but his letters were filled with reproaches for his wife's silence. Rose had received no word from her family in Trois-Ilets. Summer was drawing to an end in Noisy when Laure de la Touche appeared to deliver Alexandre's letter.

At the first words Rose turned pale and could not hold back a cry of indignation. Madame de la Touche watched with interest the growing emotion of this twenty-year-old woman over whom she had so easily triumphed. Rose managed to restrain her tears while Laure gave her news of Trois-Ilets and announced her own plans to marry a Comte Arthur Dillon, onetime governor of Saint-Christophe.

When Laure had finally left, Rose gave way to her tears and indignation. Shaking with sobs, she gave the letter to her Aunt Désirée and retired to her room.

Madame Renaudin read the letter aloud to the Marquis de Beauharnais:

"If I had written you in the first moment of my anger," Alexandre wrote, "my pen would have burned the paper. . . . Despite the fury that chokes me, I shall try to restrain myself and tell you calmly that you are, in my eyes, the vilest of creatures; that my sojourn in this country has acquainted me with your abominable conduct while you were here. . . . There is no more time for pretense. After so many crimes and atrocities, what can I think about the clouds over our marriage, about this last child born eight months and a few days after my return from Italy? I am forced to claim her as my own, but I swear by Heaven that she is the child of another; a stranger's blood flows in her veins. . . . You will realize that I must avoid a similar misfortune in the future. Make, then, your arrangements; never, never shall I place myself in a position to be betrayed by you again, and since you are the kind of woman who would fool the public if we lived under the same roof, kindly take yourself to a convent as soon as you receive my letter. This is my final word. . . ." But he added a postscript: "I expect, after this letter, not to find you in my house, and I must warn you that you will find me a tyrant if you do not follow my instructions to the letter."

Laure de la Touche came back the next day and supplied the explanations that were demanded: Gaspard de la Pagerie's family had some ruthless enemies in Fort-Royal; they had not even spared Madame Renaudin from their gossip. When Rose and Désirée insisted on more details, Laure de la Touche accused the Baronesse Tascher. As to the "facts" Alexandre had learned about his wife, they were too numerous and too positive; she preferred not to repeat them. "For the rest," she added, "you may question him directly. He will be back in Paris soon."

Toward the middle of October, Alexandre announced his return to France in a letter to his wife:

"I have learned with astonishment, upon arriving in France, that you are not yet in a convent. . . . I am unshaken in my resolve. . . . I can see no inconvenience, if you wish to return to America, in letting you take that course. . ."

He advised her not to try to change his mind, but to submit

to this separation. "And believe me, Madame," he ended, "of the two of us, you are not the more to be pitied."

Rose retired to the Convent of Pentemont on the Rue de Grenelle. She left her daughter in the care of a nurse at Noisy-le-Grand, and kept her son Eugène with her.

# 4

## The Convent of Pentemont

THE CONVENT on the Rue de Grenelle—in the very heart of
the aristocratic Faubourg Saint-Germain—founded by
Bernardine nuns, spread its gardens as far as the Rue Saint-
Dominique and offered a peaceful refuge not only for dedi-
cated women who had taken the veil, but also for some thirty
women of society who, for one reason or another, were living
in temporary retirement from the world. At little expense and
in pleasant surroundings, these women led a comfortable life,
they could go out by day as usual or receive visitors. At night
the doors closed early, but this was practically the only restric-
tion imposed on those who sought out the convent as a retreat.

To some extent, the thirty lodgers lived a life in common,
meeting constantly in the refectory, the parlor, the chapel, the
corridors; and this life, for many of the younger women, was in
effect a social discipline, providing them with the opportunities of a good finishing school—learning how to bow, speak,
and walk with grace. Needless to say, at the beginning of her
stay here—which was to last twenty months—the young
Vicomtesse de Beauharnais was in no mood to learn social
graces. She avoided the other women and, not wanting to offer
opportunity for more gossip, she confined herself to her apartments on the second floor. But she was not alone, for Madame
Renaudin had, of her own accord, decided to share her niece's

banishment from society. The spectacle of her niece's grief perhaps reminded Désirée of her own destroyed marriage; certainly she must have blamed herself for her part in Rose's misfortune by planning and bringing about the marriage with Alexandre de Beauharnais.

No doubt at the advice of Madame Renaudin, Rose had instituted a countersuit against her husband. But the machinery of law turns slowly, and it was not until one morning in December that the Vicomtesse de Beauharnais received, in the convent parlor, the King's jurisconsult for the Châtelet district in Paris, Maître Louis Joron, and asked him to register her formal complaint. She recounted to him her griefs since her arrival in France, the circumstances of her marriage and Alexandre's indifference to her, his frequent absences from home. She also included in the dossier, as evidence, the last two letters from her hubsand, filled with insulting charges and threats. These accusations, she declared, were not at all inspired by jealousy, but were deliberately aimed at throwing off a yoke that weighed heavily upon him. He had ignored, she said, the testimony of respectable people, such as her father-in-law, the Marquis de Beauharnais, who could bear witness to her honesty.

When it was learned that the Vicomtesse de Beauharnais had applied for a legal separation, all Alexandre's relatives advised him to avoid a lawsuit and settle out of court. He, at first, refused to consider this. He was enjoying his newfound freedom, living a gay life and being received in the best society, appearing at all the receptions and balls, where he had the reputation of being the finest dancer in Paris. His social activities did not prevent him from annoying his father and his wife, demanding of the former an account of guardianship, and of the latter the return of all jewels he had given her. Meanwhile, he kidnaped his little son Eugène and Rose lodged a new complaint after this outrage.

Either because of this further suit, or simply wearying of his inglorious behavior, Alexandre finally accepted a compromise. On March 4, 1785, the couple met in the office of their notary, Maître Trutat, where Alexandre acknowledged his faults and declared that the letters in question had been dictated by the passion and anger of youth. He agreed to the separation demanded by Rose.

The young wife, cleared of all suspicion, emerged triumphant from the ordeal. And she, too, was now free. Henceforth she could live wherever she liked, move about at her own inclination, manage her fortune, and draw revenues from it. The Vicomte de Beauharnais pledged himself to pay her an annual allowance of 5,000 livres to cover the costs of food, upkeep, and education of his son and daughter. Up to the age of five, it was agreed that Eugène should remain with his mother. As for Hortense, she would remain with her mother until the event of a remarriage; and, for her upkeep, there would be an additional thousand livres.

Six months later, Rose left the Convent of Pentemont to join her aunt and father-in-law in their house at Fontainebleau.

To escape the cares, torments, griefs, and wrongs of mankind and fortune, nothing could be more suitable than this town. Nothing could be more peaceful than its forest, where silence was only occasionally disturbed by the fanfares, shouting, and barking attendant upon a royal hunt. And nowhere could a more select society be found than in the châteaux surrounding the ancient and beautiful palace of the kings of France.

Frequenting this society at Fontainebleau completed the social education Marie Josèphe Rose had received during her twenty-month sojourn at Pentemont. As acquaintances, she had the Comte de Montmorin, governor of the château of Fontainebleau, Monsieur de Cheissac, deputy ranger of the King's Forest, the Vicomtesse de Bethisy, Monsieur Hue, Madame Jamin—all great names and all highly cultivated people, at whose houses one enjoyed good conversation and all the refinements of life. Gradually, the natural attributes of the young Creole—so long undefined—emerged; and her face, gestures, mien—even her language—became more graceful, charming, and noble. She was no longer the awkward little provincial girl, lacking in conversation and almost without attractions, but a woman of the world, coquettish, expressive, elegant, and tasteful in dress. Unfortunately, her taste in dress was also expensive.

Immediately after the separation, Rose had thought herself rich. The remittances from her father, added to the allowance made by Alexandre, brought her income to 11,000 livres; a sufficient amount, she thought, to live as she liked. But the allowance from Alexandre did not always come regularly. Prodigal in his pleasures, the vicomte proved to be forgetful of his obligations, and as a result, Rose soon experienced privations. Her aunt and father-in-law were living in reduced circumstances and could give her little if any aid. Madame Renaudin was ill, and the Marquis de Beauharnais's pension had been reduced by two thirds in a recent effort at economizing by the Council of State. Even more uncertain was the income drawn by Rose's father from his badly run plantations. To raise additional money, Rose and Madame Renaudin had sold the house at Noisy, but to no avail. Further economies were necessary; income from other sources must be found. The marquis and Madame Renaudin decided to sell the house on the Rue Saint-Charles, retire from Paris, and live at Fontainebleau. There, at any rate, they would be near old friends and relatives—little Hortense's godmother, the poetess Fanny (née Mouchard) de Beauharnais, among others. Their first house at Fontainebleau was on the Rue Montmorin. Then, somehow, they bought a house with a garden on the Rue de France, and it was there, in May, 1787, that Rose's eyes were opened to her financial situation.

The Baron Tascher paid a visit, bringing with him Gaspard de la Pagerie's remittance, much reduced in amount. After discussion of her father's situation and prospects, it became evident to Rose that her income from then on would be barely enough to pay off her creditors. Between her father's carelessness and the willful negligence of her husband, Rose had incurred many debts—and, admittedly, Marie Josèphe Rose would never be able to live without incurring debts.

Before leaving, the Baron Tascher suggested that Rose return to Martinique with him. Her mother had expressed an urgent desire to see her daughter and grandchildren, and in Martinique she could live much more cheaply than in France. Rose hesitated for a while but finally refused. The voyage would be costly, and she felt that Hortense was still too young for such a trip.

Perhaps with an idea of raising the funds for the proposed return to Martinique, Rose wrote to her father, asking him to send the money he owed her and explaining her pressing need. She also gave news of her children: "Hortense," she wrote, "is my great consolation. She is charming, both in looks and character. She often asks about her grandparents in Martinique, and she does not forget her Aunt Manette. 'Shall I see them soon, Mamma?' she often asks me. Eugène has been four months at a boarding school in Paris; he is in wonderful health. He was unable to be inoculated because of his second teeth which are now coming in—early for his age, since he is only seven. He is as good as his sister, and his father loves him very much. I have news of him every week and send back news of my daughter in return."

In Martinique things were going badly. Gaspard de la Pagerie was still in wretched health, and Manette was wasting away, consumed by a slow, constant fever. Grandmother de Sanois had died, and Madame de la Pagerie was alone at Trois-Ilets with the two invalids. As the year passed, Rose received many letters from her mother, urging her to return to Trois-Ilets.

By the time Hortense was five years old, Rose hesitated no longer and made her plans for the return to Martinique. Before leaving France, she had to pay off her most demanding creditors: We know that she owed 156 livres to Lanot the shoemaker; 90 livres, 10 sols to Desnos the shoemaker; 103 livres to the laundress; 1,630 livres to a certain Tardif—another tradesman, no doubt, but the details are missing. Madame Renaudin assured her that she would take care of the balance of the debts during her niece's absence, but there still remained the costs of the journey from Paris to Le Havre and the voyage from Le Havre to Martinique. To raise this amount Rose sold some of her possessions and left instructions for selling others after her departure, among them her precious harp.

Thus it was in Martinique that the first rumors of the French Revolution, which was to turn the world upside down —particularly the world in which she had learned to move— came to Rose.

Upon her arrival, there was apparently a little whirl of social events in Fort-Royal, for Rose sent requests to Madame Renaudin to forward from Paris certain articles of festive attire, among them a dozen fans. There was also the christening of a little cousin, Stéphanie Tascher de la Pagerie, whom Rose held over the baptismal font and who was destined to play a part in Rose's future. Old acquaintances had evidently forgotten the scandal created in Fort-Royal by the Vicomte de Beauharnais, for many of them entertained for her during her brief visit.

As each cargo ship and battleship brought ever grimmer news from France, however, life at Fort-Royal and Trois-Ilets became less cheerful. The news became even more detailed. The people of Paris had stormed the Bastille. The nobility and the clergy had renounced their feudal rights. The red, white, and blue tricolor was now the flag of France.

There were repercussions even in Fort-Royal. Blunders committed by the acting governor of the island, the Comte de Vioménil, increased the tension, and three companies of the

Martinique regiment and two colonial battalions mutinied. Officers who refused to wear the tricolored cockade were clubbed to death with rifle butts. In the streets of the town there were clashes between white colonials and mulattoes, who had threatened to arm the Negro slaves. Some of the plantation owners tried to get transfer for themselves and their slaves to the Spanish island of Trinidad.

For almost two years in Martinique Rose was without news of her son Eugène and Madame Renaudin. She urgently wanted to return to France, and she finally persuaded the Baron Tascher, who commanded the ports of the island, to procure passage for her. While awaiting the ship, she took refuge with seven-year-old Hortense in Government House.

On June 16, 1790, Negro rioters seized Fort Bourbon above the town, where the garrison was in revolt. Cannons were directed upon the town, and a bombardment was expected at any moment. One night, when told that the bombardment would begin at any moment, a terrified Rose took her daughter in her arms and ran down to the docks where the frigate *Sensible* was anchored. As she ran, there was a first detonation of the cannon, and bullets spattered along her line of flight.

Captain Durand d'Ubraye accommodated mother and child on his vessel, along with other refugees, and, when fired upon, weighed anchor. Untouched, after being under fire for almost an hour, the vessel rounded the Pointe des Nègres, keeping under sail at the entrance of the harbor but awaiting orders from shore. When none were forthcoming after a long delay, the *Sensible* steered a course toward France.

Storm-tossed, the frigate almost went aground in the Straits of Gibraltar, but with the united efforts of crew and passengers —we are told that even little Hortense helped—shipwreck was avoided. Two months after her departure from Fort-Royal, the *Sensible* dropped anchor in the port of Toulon.

# 5

## The Carmelite Friars

IT MUST have been a bewildering experience to step into the France of that epoch, a transitional world, no longer a monarchy but not yet a democracy. There was a whole new vocabulary to be learned. The aristocrats closest to the throne were living in exile—and scheming. They were the *émigrés*. The Friends of the Constitution who in former times had held meetings in an old Jacobin monastery were now in power, they were called the *Jacobins*.

Power for the Jacobins meant a new status for the Vicomte de Beauharnais. As a member of the Constituent Assembly, he took an active part in government, proving himself as adept a speaker as he was a dancer. Alexandre was still much sought after, and Rose occasionally met him in the *salons* she frequented. She even made some overtures toward a reconciliation, but without success. Their children were the only bond between them.

With his change of fortune, Alexandre paid her allowance regularly, and Rose was free of debts. She now wanted to have a home of her own, where she could lead a life more suitable to the graces she had acquired, and to take her place in society. As long as she lived with her Aunt Désirée, she must remain merely a spectator, not only of society at large but of her popular husband.

At the time, the Vicomte de Beauharnais was paying open court to Madame Amelot, a famous coquette who amused herself by letting Alexandre stake his charms against those of his friend, Hérault de Séchelles, another man about town of the epoch.

When the Constituent Assembly was supplanted by the Legislative Assembly in the autumn of 1791, Alexandre went back into the army. This took him away from Paris and ten-year-old Eugène, who was enrolled in the Collège d'Harcourt. Rose decided to settle in Paris, to be near both her children; Hortense was in the convent school of the Abbaye-aux-Bois of which Madame de Chabrillan was abbess. A house was found on the Rue Saint-Dominique, which Rose had decorated to her taste—a taste that was to become famous and eventually dictate fashion. She soon acquired a circle of friends, some of them people her own age whom she had known in Martinique, some of them important members of the new transitional society, among whom were several friends of Alexandre.

In Martinique she had become friendly with a rich widow named Madame Hosten. Their friendship was first based upon their children, Madame Hosten having two daughters about Hortense's age. Then, in 1791, when Rose had suffered two bereavements in the deaths of her father and her sister Manette, Madame Hosten had been a great consolation and eventually had taken Rose out into society to distract her from her grief.

In Rose's little blue and silver drawing room a glittering company often assembled: Alexandre's friends, Montesquiou, d'Aiguillon, and Hérault de Séchelles; the Prince de Salm and his sister Amalia de Hohenzollern, who became warm friends of hers; the poetess Fanny de Beauharnais, now over fifty but still alluring; the Prince de Gonzague-Castiglione; the Baron Clootz; Bitaubé, the translator of Homer; and several others well known in literary circles of the time, among them the Abbé Barthélémy, and Cubières-Palmézeaux, both great admirers of Rose. She could now hold her own in discussions of Voltaire and Rousseau with these intellectuals, who affected disdain for their titles and enthusiasm for "liberal" ideas. The Revolution was apparently becoming stagnant.

Then came August 10, 1792, and the attack on the Tuileries . . .

Rose's first thought was for her children and she immediately sent for Eugène and Hortense to keep them with her.

In the confusing weeks and months that followed, the King was imprisoned and then released; a threatened invasion of the Prussians was stopped at Valmy; a National Convention was set up to succeed the Legislative Assembly and initiate a truly republican form of government; and Rose did many foolish things.

She tried to send her children abroad and, without informing her husband, who had been appointed chief of staff of the Army of the Rhine, she entrusted them to Prince de Salm who was fleeing to England with his sister. The fugitives were stopped at Saint-Pol by Alexandre who had heard of the escapade, and had rightly judged that if it were successful it would compromise his career. The children were sent back to Rose in Paris. This and other acts of panic can be forgiven her in the face of multiplying scenes of terror in Paris. Arrests, assassinations, pillage, and conflagrations were almost daily occurrences.

Rose was not sorry to have her children for company at a time when many of her friends had left Paris or gone into hiding, and her own life was largely restricted to the four walls of her house on the Rue Saint-Dominique.

Her household at this time was comprised of two maidservants and a valet, Hortense's governess, Marie de Lannoy, and a bad-tempered pug dog named Fortuné, who bit everyone, including his mistress, and was the real master of the house.

When the Vicomte de Beauharnais was appointed general

of the Army of the Rhine, Rose, as his wife (even though legally separated), received at her house many influential men who sought her favor. Many of them were former members of the Constituent Assembly who now occupied important posts in the Convention, and through her influence with them Rose helped many of her titled friends who were in trouble. When, for example, the niece of the Marquis de Moulins, Mademoiselle de Béthisy, was thrown into prison, Rose was able, thanks to the great revolutionary, Tallien, to save her from certain death.

After the execution of Louis XVI, when England, Spain, and Holland united with Austria and Prussia to crush the Revolution, Rose's status changed. The French army suffered one defeat after another, Mainz, Condé, Valenciennes fell into the hands of the invaders, and Toulon surrendered to the English. Alexandre handed in his resignation as commander in chief and retired first to Ferté-Avrain before finally settling at Blois. "Citizeness Beauharnais" had to abdicate, too. She abandoned her charming little house on the Rue Saint-Dominique and leased a country house at Croissy, near Chatou, which had formerly been occupied by the Hosten family. There she spent the remainder of this dreadful and epoch-making year.

Meanwhile, Alexandre could not give up his political ambitions. At Chaumont, he presided over a Jacobin society; at Ferté-Avrain he set up a "revolutionary committee of surveillance." But try as he would, in his own words, to "wear himself out in schemes for the good of the Republic," to "exhaust himself in efforts for the happiness of the citizens of the Republic," he did not feel safe. Disaster struck on the twelfth of Ventôse, the sixth month [February-March] of the second year of the Republican calendar, 1794. He was arrested at Blois. The former commander in chief of the Army of the Rhine was brought to Paris, imprisoned in the Luxembourg Palace, and then transferred to the former Abbey of the Carmelite Friars, now a crowded prison, in the Rue de Vaugirard.

From that moment, Rose's only thought was to save Alexandre. She petitioned all the men in government who had helped her obtain the release of Mademoiselle de Béthisy. She had never believed she could be so brave. When Tallien told her that her husband's fate was in the hands of the terrible Vadier, then President of the Committee of Public Safety, she immediately went to see him. When she was not admitted, she wrote him a letter imploring mercy for his former associate in the Constituent Assembly. She boasted of the onetime vicomte's patriotism: "If he were not Republican, he could have neither my affection nor esteem. . . . My household is a Republican household; before the Revolution I made no distinction between my children and the *sans-culottes* of today." She flattered, and she begged: "I am asking you neither favor nor mercy, but I appeal to your sensibility and your humanity."

Less than a month later, an anonymous letter, issued from Croissy, recommended that the Committee of Public Safety beware of the onetime Vicomtesse Alexandre de Beauharnais. She was, said the anonymous writer, in close contact "with the offices of ministers" and for that reason was "dangerous." The house on the Rue Saint-Dominique was searched, and her papers were examined. Two desks and wardrobes were sealed and stored in the attic for further examination, and the next day, she was arrested.

The children were asleep, and the governess, Mademoiselle de Lannoy, wanted to wake them up. "No," Rose said, "let them sleep. I could not bear to see their tears. I would not have enough strength to leave them."

She was taken to the Prison of the Carmelite Friars. There she encountered her husband and numerous acquaintances, among them the Prince de Salm and the Duchesse d'Aiguillon. Her relations with Alexandre became more cordial. Both forgot their grudges, and even forgave each other. They became reconciled in their common peril and in their love and fear for their children.

In a report drawn up for the Committee of Public Safety, Alexandre demanded his liberty. He appealed for recognition of his "democratic services," offered to "increase the hatred of kings" in the hearts of his children, and pointed out that his twelve-and-a-half-year-old son was learning "the craft of cabinetmaking," and that his daughter, aged eleven, had been "raised according to Republican principles."

An order had, in effect, been issued that young nobles must learn a craft or trade. Every morning Eugène reported to a cabinetmaker in his Paris quarter, an ardent Jacobin who boasted of having taken the hammer of Louis XVI during the storming of the Tuileries.

Hortense and Eugène sent necessities to their mother in prison, and sometimes came to see her in the afternoons. But how could they communicate their thoughts? How could they receive letters from her, or send reassuring letters in return? All their interviews were closely watched.

Mademoiselle de Lannoy, the governess, was the one who thought up a clever means of transmitting notes and petitions being drawn up in Rose's behalf by a faithful friend, Monsieur Calmelet. The dog Fortuné played the principal role; his collar provided a convenient hiding place. While fondling the little dog, Rose discovered the notes, which, though brief, kept her somewhat informed of the well-being of her loved ones outside the prison walls.

The conditions inside the prison walls are well recorded in history. The prisoners slept where they could, in unlighted corridors filled with the stench of the latrines, or in cells where the windows were either walled up or set high and darkened by heavy bars. The walls of the prison were still red in places from the blood of the Carmelite monks who had been massacred the previous September. The prisoners wandered wretchedly through this constant twilight. The women's short skirts soon took on the same nondescript coloring. They could make no effort at coquetry in their dress. The men let their beards grow and went about in shirt sleeves and short breeches with bared legs. They protected their heads from the chill with kerchiefs. Their bodies were devoured by lice. They consoled themselves with love affairs, and one of the prisoners, the fifteen-year-old Mademoiselle Croiseille, became pregnant.

Rose soon noticed that Alexandre was avoiding her to spend his time with the beautiful Delphine de Custine. Rebuffed by her husband, Rose sought comfort in another man's admiration. He was the young and handsome General Hoche who slept in the cell adjacent to the one she shared with the Duchesse d'Aiguillon. The friendship was brought about by chance, for in order to go anywhere from his own cell, General Hoche had to go through the young women's cell. He was only twenty-six years old, and when he was transferred to the Conciergerie, Rose, deprived of any solace, was in total despair.

There was one meal a day, a first serving for the men and a second one for the women. The aristocratic prisoners were constantly subjected to the scornful jeering of their guards, and their personal effects—blankets and clothing—were often rifled.

From time to time a prisoner would be led away, never to be seen again. Cut off from communication with the world, the remaining prisoners circulated chance rumors and lived in a constant state of tension and dreadful expectancy.

In the fourth month of Alexandre de Beauharnais's imprisonment, a rumor spread that threw everyone into a panic. The guards laughed and talked loudly about the good old days of 1792 that were going to be repeated because of a "prison plot." The prisoners knew what this meant for them—their heads would fall . . .

A few weeks later, on the fourth of Thermidor [July-August], Alexandre was led away between two guards, and taken to the dread Conciergerie. After his interrogation, he wrote a touching letter to Rose. He was aware, he said, of the fate that awaited him, and was entrusting his children to his wife. "My tender affection for them," he wrote, "the fraternal attachment that binds me to you, can leave no doubt in your mind as to the feelings with which I shall leave this life. . . . Farewell, I embrace you, as I embrace my beloved children, for a last time . . ."

Next day the executioner led him, with forty-four other condemned prisoners, to the Place du Trône-Renversé, where the guillotine stood.

Rose was not informed of his death until the morning of the ninth, and her outburst of tears was followed by black despair. For days she refused to be comforted, and the Duchesse d'Aiguillon gently reproached her for weeping over a man who had made her suffer so much, and from whom she herself wanted to be separated.

"I had reasons," said Marie Josèphe Rose, "for being attached to my husband that make me mourn his loss."

That night the guard locked her cell earlier than usual. Believing that her husband's fate was also in store for her, she spent a night of terror, listening to all the sounds that drifted in from the street through the thick walls. First there was the sounding of an alarm, then a hue and cry, and the hurrying footsteps of crowds of people, whose shouts grew louder and louder. There were noisy proclamations, but the words were indistinguishable.

By six o'clock the next evening the news was out: The Commune had fallen, and Robespierre had been arrested and executed. The prisoners had escaped massacre by a hair's breadth. For two days the head of the police, Grépin, had been stationed outside the door of the Carmelite Prison, waiting for the order to execute all prisoners. But in the confusion of the rioting no orders had been forthcoming.

There was an explosion of joy throughout the prison—laughing, weeping, embracing, and hymn singing. The rejoicing increased when it was learned that henceforth the door to the gardens would be left open, and the prisoners would be allowed to write and receive letters, to communicate with the outside world.

Nine days later Citizeness Beauharnais was freed. She knew that her friend Jean Tallien, president of the Convention at the time of her arrest, was exerting every effort in her behalf; but when her name was called out, she fainted, so great was her emotion.

# 6

## The Widow of the Vicomte de Beauharnais

Paris, Brumaire 30, Year III

To Madame de la Pagerie, at her home in Trois-Ilets, Martinique

Dear Mamma:

Someone who is leaving for New England has kindly offered to send this letter to you. No doubt you have heard of my misfortune; I have now been widowed for four months. My only remaining consolations are my children, and you, dear mother. . . .

IT WAS AN appeal for help, discreet but painful.

Upon leaving the Prison of the Carmelites, Rose found herself without resources, with two children to feed and clothe, debts to be settled, and no friends or relatives to whom she could turn. The Marquis de Beauharnais and Madame Renaudin, ruined by inflated money, by the withdrawal of pensions and destruction of properties, could be counted on for nothing. The young and ardent General Hoche had been appointed to the command of the Army of the West, and left for Vendée shortly after his release from prison; he had been freed two days before Rose. He offered to take Eugène, who was now thirteen, with him and teach him to be a soldier. Rose shed many tears before she agreed to part from her son, but now it was an accomplished fact, and she must frantically seek more ways to reduce her expenses and pay her debts.

English ships were plowing the Atlantic and stopping all traffic with the West Indies. Rose no longer received money from Trois-Ilets, and she could not touch her late husband's property.

Since her return to France, Rose had been helped by a banker from Dunkirk, a Monsieur Emmery, who was an old friend of the Taschers. For three years he had been advancing her money, but he might die, or grow weary of lending without security. Then, how would she manage to live?

On the twelfth of Nivôse, that same year, Rose again wrote to her mother: "Without the kind attentions of my good friend Emmery and his associate Monsieur Vanhée, I do not know what would become of me. I am too confident of your affection to doubt in the least that you will make every effort to procure the means of living for me and enable me to pay off my debt to Monsieur Emmery."

Upon his advice, she directed Madame de la Pagerie to send any available funds to London or Hamburg. From there they could be transmitted to Emmery and Vanhée.

Meanwhile, in the Rue Saint-Dominique, life was penurious. The faithful servants worked without wages; they even offered to give their savings to Rose, but this was little reassurance. How could the future be secured with rising inflation? For a bunch of radishes one must hand out a fistful of promissory notes. A short ride in a fiacre cost 600 livres, which, before the Revolution, would have taken care of almost a month's living expenses. A fan and one dress cost 20,000 livres—what Rose's entire trousseau had cost, a little more than thirteen years before—and for two packets of candles one paid 2,000 livres.

There was misery everywhere, with rioting for bread, and people were dying of hunger. Even water was scarce; a bottle of water cost more than a bottle of wine.

While there was rioting and dying in the streets, agitators, profiteers, and a few people with well-invested fortunes were dancing, gaming, and feasting. Financial speculation was rampant, and everyone became a trader. Homes were turned into veritable bazaars, where every chair was piled high with parcels of sugar, rolls of cloth, and boxes of lace. Storerooms were emptied of everything that could be exchanged. Men of all classes were infected with the same fever. Everything was bought and sold—coffee, jewels, shoes, gun carriages, paintings, bronze statuettes. Respectable and not-so-respectable women became merchants and jobbers. Laden with samples of their wares, they stopped passers-by in the street, offering to sell tobacco, soap, salt, gloves, and handkerchiefs. "Nothing was repugnant to their delicate fingers.... The prettiest hands wallowed in leather, suet, and butter. Venus, like the Roman emperor, found the smell of money sweet."

For more than a year, Rose struggled without respite against poverty. Returning friends and new acquaintances obliged her to keep up a certain style of living. It was unthinkable that she might one day have to stand in line at the door of the baker or the butcher, as did the poor people. She was convinced she had been born to enjoy the finer things of life, and even more sure of it whenever she met again the elegant women she had known at Pentemont, the Carmelites, or at Fanny's. She had set up close friendships with many of them.

She began selling off silk stockings and fine lingerie, first finding customers in the *salons* where she was received, but ending up by searching people out in their homes and badgering them into making purchases.

She continued to submit petition after petition to those in power, and at last, thanks to Tallien and Merlin de Thionville, the official seals were removed from her possessions in the Rue Saint-Dominique. Once more she could enjoy her fine clothes, jewels, and furniture, and her children's personal effects. Through a representative of the government "on a mission" to the Loire valley, she obtained the restitution of her silverware, which had been seized at La Ferté-Avrain after Alexandre's arrest. Madame Renaudin, after the sale of her house at Fontainebleau, was able to pay her taxes for the Year IV. In payment for the carriages her husband had abandoned to the Army of the Rhine, the Committee of Public Safety allotted her a carriage and two black Hungarian horses.

But in spite of these loans and restitutions, Rose still owed money everywhere. Generous and spendthrift, she did not know how to limit either her expenses or her charities. There came a day when she found herself obliged to draw one thousand pounds sterling from her mother.

Because of her generosity people took an added interest in her misfortune. It was known that when Alexandre's elder brother François had emigrated to England, Rose took charge of his daughter Émilie. Such generous acts had increased her expenses, but now they occasionally lightened her misfortunes. It was the custom, for example, in these difficult times, that each guest should bring his own bread when invited out to dine. An exception was made in Rose's favor when she dined at the homes of Madame de Moulins, Madame Hosten, or the latter's son-in-law, Monsieur de Croiseuil. Rose had saved Madame de Moulins's niece from the guillotine, and both Madame Hosten and her son-in-law owed their liberation from the Prison of the Carmelites to her. In these homes she was surrounded by every kind attention, but nowhere was she made to feel more at home than at the Talliens'. The Talliens were her closest and most valuable friends.

Rose had a great deal in common with beautiful young Thérésa Tallien. Their similar personalities and life histories drew them together: Both were outgoing and generous, and women of taste and elegance; both had made unfortunate early marriages to men far too young for them, and who had betrayed them. Thérésa's first husband, the Marquis de Fontenay, had behaved with her exactly as Beauharnais had with Rose.

A month after her divorce, Thérésa had been arrested at Robespierre's decree and imprisoned at the Petite-Force. Her execution was ordered and she was about to climb the scaffold, when Tallien (no doubt in great part because he had fallen madly in love with Thérésa) provoked the fall of the tyrant on the ninth of Thermidor. It was to Tallien's beautiful wife that the people of France and Paris felt they owed their freedom from fear, and they bestowed upon her the name of Our Lady of Thermidor. During the Terror, when Tallien had been sent by the Convention into the department of the Gironde and made Bordeaux tremble, Thérésa had saved many aristocrats and humble folks from the guillotine. She was still able to hand out favors, for Tallien was now an important member of the Committees of Public Safety and General Security.

Thérésa was only twenty-two years old, ten years younger than Rose; her hair and eyes were dark, while Rose's eyes were hazel and her hair auburn. They were foils for each other's beauty, and perhaps the difference in age helped eliminate the possibility of their becoming rivals as leaders of fashion in Paris.

On the evening of her marriage to Tallien—the sixth of Nivôse, Year III—Thérésa entertained for the first time at their charming house which they called "the cottage," *La Chaumière*. It was set among lilacs and poplars at the corner of Cours-la-Reine and the Allée des Veuves, a veritable comic-opera cottage. The guests included ancient titles such as the Duchesse d'Aiguillon's, and great writers and statesmen like the Vicomte de Barras and Marie Joseph Chénier.

Barras was then approaching forty. Imposing of stature, handsome of face, a noted wit and epicurean, he was living apart from his wife and was much sought after in all the *salons*. When it was known that the widowed Vicomtesse de Beauharnais had taken a house in the Chaussée-d'Antin quarter at ten thousand francs' rent, some people declared that she was the mistress of this all-powerful member of the Convention. Had he not restored her husband's property to her? Had he not advised her to put her daughter in boarding school—perhaps to get rid of an embarrassing witness?

It was true that Rose had placed Hortense with Madame Campan, who had been a lady in waiting of Marie Antoinette and now kept a school in Saint-Germain. But Hortense at the age of twelve would properly have been at some such school, and this one happened to be not far from Monsieur MacDermott's Collège Irlandais which Eugène, called back from the army by his mother, now attended.

But it must be confessed that Rose's way of life during this period could easily provoke gossip.

Her house was at No. 6, Rue Chantereine, near the Ouvrard Bank. Its white façade could be seen at the end of a hundred-yard-long, tree-lined avenue, surrounded by gardens, with stables and outbuildings. There were two stories above a basement floor, and a double flight of steps led up to the porch. From a vestibule one entered a dining room with French windows, and beyond that was a bedroom and a semi-circular drawing room. It was a tiny but charming dwelling, on which the Vicomtesse de Beauharnais lavished her exquisite taste and no doubt a great deal of money.

She received her guests in the dining room. The little drawing room was used as a boudoir-dressing room. The bedroom was furnished with a small couch, its woodwork ornamented with bronze, and six chairs with inverted backs, covered with blue nankeen, edged with red and yellow braid. Mingled with the new furnishings were fine pieces from the house on the Rue Saint-Dominique: an octagonal table in light wood with a marble top; a writing table in Guadeloupe walnut; a secretary in citron wood ornamented with red wood; a marble bust of Socrates; a pouch table; and a harp. The boudoir contained a pianoforte, several prints on the walls, and above all mirrors.

There were mirrors over the fireplace, on the dressing table, and on a chest of drawers.

While the little house in Paris was being prepared, Rose received her friends at Croissy. Her house there was within view of that of Étienne Denis Pasquier, councilor of the Paris Parliament, and in his monumental memoirs we find descriptions of some of the parties Rose gave at this time, particularly in the summer season when Pasquier and his wife lived at their country retreat. Once a week they would see quantities of baskets arrive, filled with food, and shortly afterward the carriages from Paris would bring the Talliens, Paul de Barras, and many other distinguished guests. Since he and his wife were also entertained by the Vicomtesse de Beauharnais, Pasquier could describe the game, the fruit, and the other rare foods that were served at her table, all contributions of her guests in this time of want. But, though there were exotic foods, there was still a lack of many bare necessities, and not infrequently Rose would borrow from the Pasquiers a saucepan, plates, or glasses.

When Barras entertained in his house on the Rue Basse-Pierre, Rose acted as hostess for him, but whether there was anything more to the gossip of the times has never been proved. It was in his house that she was eventually to meet General Bonaparte, a meeting brought about largely by Thérésa Tallien.

For months before she met Bonaparte, Rose heard both Barras and Thérésa talk about the little, twenty-six-year-old general. Barras regarded him as his protégé, and at the same time spoke of him with great admiration. They had met at the siege of Toulon, where Bonaparte had accomplished marvels; but for some time now the talented young officer had been on half pay and living in want and anxiety. He was often seen in the streets of Paris, a haggard little man, followed by his aides-de-camp, Marmont and Junot, who were as famished looking as he. Madame Tallien had taken an interest in him, and invited him often to her home. She even gave him some cloth for a new uniform, when she saw that his old one was threadbare.

Rose listened indifferently to all the talk about Bonaparte and seemed to have no interest in meeting him, even when Thérésa assured her she would be "struck by the expression in his eyes. He is very clever, and knows how to predict your future by reading the lines of your hands. I will introduce you to him."

Ever since that "terrible mill of silence," the guillotine, had stilled Robespierre's harsh voice, the Jacobins had been harried and driven underground by organized bands of counter-revolutionaries, who called themselves the Muscadins. Their headquarters were at the Palais-Égalité—formerly known as the Palais-Royal—and their uniform consisted of checked coats, green cravats, tight breeches, and blond wigs. This band of turbulent youths was drawn from every walk of life. Store-keepers, bank employees, office workers, and attorneys' clerks rubbed elbows with titled *émigrés* who had returned to France. Their leaders were Tallien, Legendre, Fréron, and their queen was the beautiful Thérésa. They organized demonstrations, tore down Jacobin propaganda, and suppressed terrorist riots with clubs and bludgeons. They had saved the Convention, and now, in the summer of 1795, they wanted to make its laws. The counter-revolution was completely out of hand, and the Convention seemed to be lost. The situation became critical in the month of Vendémiaire [October-November] with almost constant demonstrating in the streets of Paris. The Convention placed Barras in charge of the defense forces, and on the night of the twelfth, he called upon General Bonaparte to help him.

Bonaparte had the artillery, which happened to be at Sablons, brought immediately to Paris by Murat. They occupied the approaches to the Tuileries, and from the steps of the church of Saint-Roch, fired on the packed crowd. In a few hours the rebels had dispersed, and the next day General Bonaparte was the new hero of the Republic with the nickname of General Vendémiaire.

Two days later the Convention met for a last time to dissolve itself and appoint a Directory of five members to take over executive power. The legislative power was assigned to two chambers: the Council of Five Hundred (*Les Cinq-Cents*) and the Council of the Ancients. The Ancients met in the Tuileries; the Five Hundred in the Salle du Manège; and the Directory—Barras, Carnot, Letourneur, Rewbell, La Revellière-Lépeaux—established themselves in the Luxembourg Palace.

While the first floor of the Luxembourg Palace was being furnished for him, Barras entertained lavishly at his house on the Rue Basse-Pierre, with Thérésa Tallien, who had recently become his favorite, as hostess. He greeted his guests with one arm around her waist. A bevy of beautiful women, bare-shouldered and bare-bosomed, was always present, among them the young Madame Récamier, Madame de Château-Renault, and the Vicomtesse de Beauharnais. The ugly but charming Madame Hamelin was always present too, flashing her black eyes and uttering her daring bons mots which had earned her the reputation of being "the bawdiest raconteur in France." There was dancing, conversation, and card games—faro, whist, bouillotte—for diversion; and the hero of the hour, General Vendémiaire.

Now named commander in chief of the Army of the Interior, Bonaparte possessed money, horses, carriages. Yesterday, scorned and obscure; today, he was much sought after, entertained, and demanded in society. His duties obliged him to appear at the directors' homes, and he often dined at Carnot's or shared the black soup of the virtuous La Revellière-Lépeaux; but most often he was to be found at the home of Paul Barras.

It was there that he first met the Vicomtesse de Beauharnais.

That evening she was wearing a gown of Indian mousseline de soie. Her round, firm arms were bare below short puff sleeves and on her shoulders were two curiously wrought jewels —lion heads in enamel. When Bonaparte was presented to her, she at once made him sit beside her, and made some flattering remarks upon his military talents. At first he was shy, but she soon put him at ease by asking for details of the affair of the thirteenth of Vendémiaire and the capture of Toulon. She had a way of listening with her head to one side, her eyes beneath their long lashes looking intently into the eyes of the speaker. Bonaparte was charmed. She found him handsome despite his angular features, olive complexion, and hollow cheeks. The harmonious curve of his forehead, the arched brows, the sharp line of the imperious nose, the energetic chin, all reminded her of the profiles of Roman emperors on the gold medals her old friend, the Marquis de Caulaincourt, had given her.

Encouraged and put at ease by her interest, Bonaparte answered her questions, and was soon even telling her his childhood memories. He was enthralled by her quiet charm, by the gentle vibrations of her voice, softened still more by her musical Creole pronunciation. Bonaparte would soon be twenty-seven. Despite his austere upbringing, his wild and solitary adolescence, Bonaparte had not been indifferent to women. But his sentimental involvements had been only a few trifling affairs or light flirtations that poverty had prevented him from pursuing further. Never had a woman produced in him the emotion he felt as he sat beside the Vicomtesse de Beauharnais. Barras's *salon* was filled that night with young and beautiful women, but he saw only Rose, heard only her voice. Her least word or gesture delighted him, and he was happier than he had ever been. Soon he was paying her compliments on her hair and dress, which surrounded her like a cloud, lightly accenting the grace of her movements.

By his look of adoration, Rose saw at once that General Bonaparte found her pleasing ... very pleasing. He was conquered. With a moving, grateful smile she invited him to lunch the next day at her house on the Rue Chantereine.

# General Bonaparte Comes to Call

THE GENERAL arrived before the appointed hour. Gonthier, the butler, showed him into the dining room, where a table covered with a voluminous damask cloth was set for four. He had time, while awaiting his hostess, to examine and admire the room.

Four walnut chairs, upholstered in black horsehair, were drawn up to the table. Firelight gleamed on plates of blue and white porcelain and crystal wine glasses. Garlands of fresh flowers surrounded decanters of wine and bowls of rare fruit. There was no sound in the room except the crackling of the wood fire. Bonaparte wandered about, examining the prints that hung above two walnut side tables. One drawing particularly caught his attention: it represented a frightened child, huddled against a woman with generous breasts, whose forehead was bound with a ribbon, and who brandished a sword in her right hand. Two tall cupboards were set in the wall, and on the shelves a tea urn of Etruscan design, platters, and vases flashed their fine silver. The windows of the room opened out upon the garden, white with snow.

Bonaparte was charmed by the simplicity of the room where nothing was done to impress, where everything denoted restraint and taste, and where an aura of the old regime seemed to hover like perfume. That old world, noble and brilliant, was the world of the vicomtesse, and against his will Bonaparte felt himself drawn to it.

The door opened, and Madame de Beauharnais appeared. She was wearing a simple, unadorned tea gown, but it was close-fitting and showed off her lithe, supple form better than her voluminous skirts of the night before. Bonaparte kissed her hand as Gonthier announced the two other guests, Rose's old friends, the former Marquis de Caulaincourt and General de Ségur. Immediately after the introductions, they sat down to lunch.

Bonaparte seemed to be preoccupied and ill at ease, and said almost nothing during the meal. It was only after the departure of the other guests, when the vicomtesse asked him to stay on awhile, that he relaxed.

She showed him around the house, through her bedroom and dressing room, saying, with an apologetic smile, that it was small but pleasant, and large enough for a woman living alone.... Her children were in boarding schools. Bonaparte scarcely listened, dazed by her nearness and the intoxicating air of refinement that filled her home.

Rose asked about his brother Lucien whom she had met the previous night at Barras's house. He had seemed to her a man of intelligence and wit. How old was he? ... Only twenty? He seemed mature for his age.... Rose had actually been repelled by the gangling, nearsighted Lucien and his fixed smile, but no one would have suspected it.

Happy to talk about his family, Bonaparte became animated, gestured broadly, and broke into laughter at times for no apparent reason. He described the town of Ajaccio where he was born, in August, 1769, the second in a family of eight. Joseph, the eldest, and Lucien, the third, were both married. Then came Elisa, who would soon be nineteen. Louis had been born a year later, followed by Pauline, Caroline, and Jérôme, aged respectively fifteen, thirteen, and eleven.

The general spoke affectionately of his father and mother.

Madame Letizia, his mother, had been celebrated for her beauty, and was still beautiful, a strong, proud, courageous, and high-spirited woman. She still pronounced his name, Corsican fashion, "Napolioné." But for that matter, his family name was really Buonaparte, and his father Carlo Buonaparte had always written and pronounced it so. It was his father who had wanted him to have a career in France, but he had died a few months before Bonaparte graduated from the École Militaire of Paris.

Commissioned second lieutenant, he had spent several years in Valence, then in Auxonne, on garrison duty, learning the use of modern artillery, working from early morning till late at night, and eating only one meal a day. He had had to economize, in order to help his family. He had assumed the responsibility of bringing up and educating his brother Louis. He even cooked meals for himself and his brother—he mentioned particularly his beef stew. They lived without friends except their books, shutting in their poverty, he said. In 1793, following the troubles provoked in Corsica by the followers of Pasquale Paoli, the family house was burned down, and the Bonapartes embarked for France. Since then, what an eventful life they had led! Especially his own up to the time when the Convention had called upon him to put down the insurrection . . .

Warming to his subject as he talked, Bonaparte paced up and down, gesticulating. Fortuné, the little pug dog, circled round him constantly, growling and showing his teeth every time General Bonaparte approached the vicomtesse or seemed about to lay his hand on her arm. Stuffed with food, the dog fell asleep but soon woke up again, growling. Suddenly he leaped at the general, who flung him off, staring at him fixedly. Beneath the eyes of Bonaparte, the fierce little creature wavered, then became silent and still.

Madame de Beauharnais took the dog upon her knees, murmuring reproaches. "I cannot cure him of his ferocity," she said, apologetically, stroking her pet. "He bites everyone, even dogs larger than himself. He'll end up by being killed. I ought to get rid of him, but I can't bring myself to do it. During the Terror, while I was imprisoned, it was Fortuné that enabled me to correspond with my children and friends. . . ." And she told Bonaparte how the children's governess had concealed notes beneath the dog's collar.

She then begged Bonaparte to continue his story, which the dog had so rudely interrupted . . .

When Barras had called upon him to put down the insurrection, he had been on the point of leaving France for Turkey, to reorganize the sultan's artillery. Rose expressed surprise. He explained in clipped tones that it was in France's interest that the military organization of Turkey be strengthened. "On several occasions," he said, "that great power has asked France for artillery officers. I was without employment, so I volunteered my services . . ."

"And now," said Rose, "I hope you no longer plan to leave?"

The expression on her face and the timbre of her voice were so caressing that Bonaparte could not help smiling.

"Now," he said, "my headquarters are in Paris, Rue Neuve-des-Capucines."

Rose brought the conversation back to his family.

"From now on," he said, "they shall lack nothing. Joseph will be consul, Lucien will be commissary of war. As for Louis, who is clever and active, I shall make him my aide-de-camp."

He would plan for the others later on. Pauline had been asked in marriage several times, but unfortunately her suitors were either without fortune or morality. Bonaparte had rejected all of them, even Barras's friend Fréron.

Rose suggested that he place Caroline and Jérôme at the boarding schools where her own children were. Hortense would welcome Caroline as a sister; so would Émilie de Beauharnais, who was likewise at Madame Campan's. And Jérôme would find in Eugène a brother and friend.

The afternoon wore on, and still they had not run out of

conversation. Bonaparte had apparently forgotten that he was to have dictated some notes to Fain, his secretary. And yet the subject of those notes was uppermost in his mind, for he told Rose about them: He was drawing up a plan for the invasion of Italy, a plan he had promised to submit to the Directory without delay. He confessed his hope that the command of the Army of Italy, then under the weak General Scherer, would be entrusted to him. Bonaparte's voice became lower, more intimate.

She returned his confidences with some of her own, and described her circle of friends, the people he would meet at her house—for he would come back again, wouldn't he? She hoped so, now that they were friends. He would find that her circle of acquaintances resembled in no way the set to be encountered at Madame Tallien's or at Barras's. It included no bankers, no politicians, no very young people. And she named as her most intimate friends a number of aristocrats of the *ancien régime:* Madame de Lameth, the Duchesses d'Aiguillon and de la Gallissonnière, the Marquis de Ségur, the Marquis de Caulaincourt, Monsieur de Montesquiou, the Duc de Nivernais. . . . He would find them all pleasant company. Oh, of course, there were sometimes "outsiders." But when they had gone, she confessed that sometimes she and her friends, after making quite sure that all doors and windows were tightly shut, talked wistfully of the court of Versailles. General Bonaparte did not seem to be shocked . . .

Nothing could mar their mood of happy understanding. Words were no longer necessary. They stopped talking, as if drugged by the heat of the log fire, beside which they were sitting. Their eyes met constantly, lingered, and did not turn away. They smiled, and Rose saw again in Bonaparte's eyes the tender admiration that had charmed her the night before.

Three weeks passed for Rose without a word or sign from General Bonaparte. Why had he not returned to the house on the Rue Chantereine? She tried to find excuses for him: no doubt he was not very experienced in matters of love, not very daring with women. He had not communicated with her, yet Rose believed she had read in his eyes a kind of avowal. And for her part, had she not shown that she found him not unpleasing? Could he have forgotten her? Had someone gossiped about her to him? Had they told him about her relationship with Barras, and if so, what had they told him? Now that Bonaparte was a hero everyone was flocking around him. Rose thought with resentment of women who had the advantages of youth and fortune that she did not have. Well, she would find out what was keeping him away. The best thing to do was to write to him directly. She sat down at once and wrote him the following brief note of encouragement:

You no longer come to see a lady who is your good friend; you have dropped her completely. This is very wrong of you, for she is very fond of you.

Come tomorrow, *Septidi*,* to lunch with me. I need to see you and have a chat about your interests.

Good night, my friend.

Affectionately yours,
The Widow Beauharnais

The sixth of Brumaire

It is easy to imagine with what care she dressed for their next meeting, with what attention she masked the small imperfections of her skin with cosmetics, studying herself in the mirror, shaping her sweet, small mouth into a smile that would hide her bad teeth.

Bonaparte told her what he had written in his reply to her invitation: His work had prevented him from returning sooner. No one could want her friendship more than he, and he would do everything to prove it. His formal tone surprised and

---

* The seventh day of the Republican calendar's ten-day week.

bothered her but she concealed her feelings, and thanked him for responding so promptly to her note. Then, in her most seductive voice, she made those simple, serious, and affectionate remarks that could set hearts pounding. He forgot the reserve he had imposed upon himself and became again the man who had pleased and attracted her, amiable and expansive.

He returned the next day and all the following days, became each day more enamored and daring. Rose was wholly aware that she would end by yielding to him, and she put up only the weak defense of coquetry. Now and then he reproached her for some of her friendships, her relations with Barras, her constant presence at his receptions, which he said were attended by fawning swindlers and adventurers.

Then came the day when Bonaparte declared he would no longer call her Rose, as her friends did. Of her three Christian names, Marie Josèphe Rose, he selected the one that no one else had used, modifying it affectionately.

For him, Bonaparte, she would henceforth be Josephine.

# Part II

## JOSEPHINE, WIFE OF NAPOLEON BONAPARTE
### (1796-1804)

# 1

## *Rose Becomes Josephine*

ON THE first day of Pluviôse, Year IV [January 21, 1796], Barras gave a large dinner party at the Luxembourg Palace to celebrate an important anniversary: the execution of Louis XVI. Josephine, as her friends were learning to call her, brought her two children. Hortense, who was making her first appearance in society, was seated at table between her mother and General Bonaparte, and attracted much admiring attention. At the age of thirteen, she was "fresh as a flower," with large blue eyes, a pink and white complexion, and fair silky hair that caught the light and seemed to reflect it down upon her face. Only General Bonaparte paid no attention to the young girl's beauty, scarcely addressing a remark to her, although she was seeing him for the first time and must have turned her eyes upon him more than once. Bonaparte was completely absorbed in his conversation with Josephine, and constantly leaned across Hortense toward her, forcing the girl back in her chair.

The general's marked attentions to Madame de Beauharnais escaped no one's attention, and soon all Paris was gossiping, so much so that Barras, one day, frankly advised Bonaparte to marry Josephine. Barras assured the general he would not be refused.

When Josephine heard Bonaparte's suggestion of marriage,

65

she expressed surprise. "Why marry?" she asked. "Aren't we happy the way we are?" And to the general's, Barras's, and everyone else's amazement, she resisted the proposal.

Finally, thinking he had found a way to make her change her mind, Barras said he would ask the Directory to give Bonaparte the command of the Army of Italy. He was sure the others—La Revellière-Lépeaux and Carnot particularly—would not oppose it. Carnot had spoken with admiration of the plan the young general had submitted for driving the Austrians out of Piedmont.

All her most intimate friends urged Josephine to "marry and settle down." Monsieur Calmelet took a particularly active role in trying to make her change her status. In these difficult times, he said, she needed a husband. Bonaparte would act as father to her children, who needed a father. She had creditors: Bonaparte would pay them off. She loved society and luxury: this marriage would give her all that. She was a coquette: married, she could continue to be a coquette, with impunity. And everyone said that Bonaparte was going to be given the command of an army.

She listened to these persuasive arguments on every side. The old Marquis de Caulaincourt, who considered Bonaparte an exceptional man, advised her to conclude the marriage as soon as possible. Stroking the watch chain hung with fobs and seals that lay upon his waistcoat, he predicted the great deeds that Bonaparte would perform. "You're right," said the Marquis de Ségur, "that little general may well become a great man."

When Madame de Beauharnais reported all this to her notary, Maître Raguideau, he raged with indignation. What! The Vicomtesse de Beauharnais would consider marrying a military man, an adventurer with a sword? "What folly!" he exclaimed. "You assure me he is going to leave for Italy. But can you be sure he will be victorious where Dumerbion, Kellermann, and Scherer have failed? And if he, too, fails, what kind of future will you have? Better to marry a merchant of arms who could give you all the money you need!"

In her state of irresolution, Josephine pondered Bonaparte's motives. Was it possible that he was urging her to marry him because he thought she was rich? He had seen her dresses of taffeta, organdy, embroidered lawn, costly mousseline. But he didn't know, for instance, that she owned only six petticoats, two dozen handkerchiefs, and a dozen pairs of silk stockings. And he did not know how she dined when alone: off earthenware dishes, set on threadbare tablecloths.

Her children encouraged her in her resistance. Whenever Eugène and Hortense came home from their schools in Saint-Germain, they implored their mother not to consider marrying again. "You won't love us as much," they declared.

Shaken by their ingenuous jealousy, Josephine could not make up her mind. And there were other things to consider. Did she really love the "little Corsican"? She could not say. Did she love him with a real love? No, without doubt she did not! Did she have an aversion for him, then? No, but surely love was something more absorbing and exclusive than the feeling she had for him. In his presence, she did not feel the prescribed thrill and exaltation of her whole being that passionate lovers talked about. He had charm, yes; an irresistible charm when he smiled. But when he talked excitedly and forgot himself, what bluntness of language and gesture!

She analyzed his good and bad qualities. She admired his courage, his knowledge, his wit and understanding; his mind was so keen and penetrating that he guessed the thoughts of others before they were expressed. He recounted funny stories as marvelously well as he did ghost stories. He knew how to make one laugh; he was "droll."

But everything else about him was on too large a scale for her. His overpowering will clashed with her Creole nonchalance. His piercing eyes—his flashing eyes that seemed to look through you, burning into your soul—intimidated her.

His ambition made her afraid. Had he not said, when he heard of the promises made by Carnot and Barras, that he did not need anyone's protection? Had he not said that his sword was enough, and that he would go far with it? Even his passion frightened her. Always, at the very moment when she was about to say the expected "Yes," it was his feverish passion that stopped her.

Then, too, she had been independent for a long time; she dreaded marrying again. She had been so unhappy in her first marriage, had suffered so much from Beauharnais. It would be necessary to change her tastes and habits. She was extravagant; Bonaparte was thrifty. She was careless of the future; he loved plans and order. And then, was there not too great a difference in their age?

In her confused state of mind she wrote to a friend: "Having passed my first youth, can I hope to keep for long this violent, almost delirious love which the general shows for me? And if, after marriage, he ceased to love me, would he not regret what he had done and wish he had made a more brilliant marriage? What shall I reply to him? I could weep. . . . But that's no solution!"

But nothing could deter Bonaparte. When Josephine mentioned her age, he intoned in a shrill falsetto a song that had recently been published in the *Almanach des Grâces:*

*Believe me, when you always know how to please,*
*You are never more than twenty . . .**

Josephine's friend Calmelet renewed his arguments when he heard that Bonaparte had been appointed commander in chief of the Army of Italy. Time was pressing. Her age? They would lie a little about that.

In April she finally gave in. Calmelet and another friend of

---

* The lines of the ditty in French are:
  *Crois-moi, quand on sait toujours plaire*
  *On n'a jamais plus de vingt ans . . .*

Josephine, a certain Lesourd, appeared before a notary; Calmelet certified that he had known for such-and-such-a-time Marie Josèphe Rose Tascher de la Pagerie, widow of Citizen Beauharnais, that she had been born in Martinique in the Windward Islands, and that it was impossible to procure her birth certificate because of the English occupation of the island.

Thus, Josephine was able to declare at the registry office that she was born June 23, 1767, which made her four years younger.

The marriage contract was signed on the eighteenth of Ventôse, Year IV [March 8, 1796], in the law office of Maître Raguideau, and provided for property settlement in the following terms: "Each shall retain his or her own property; she shall retain her separate legal rights after marriage ... a legacy of fifteen hundred livres out of income shall be accorded to the future wife by the future husband should she survive him, and, in that event, she shall also be entitled to take from the estate other property which she can demonstrate belongs to her."

The marriage was set for the following day at ten o'clock in the evening, a civil ceremony carried out by Monsieur Le Clercq, the duly constituted official of the second *arrondissement* of Paris.

Bonaparte was late. Three of the witnesses, Barras, Tallien, and Calmelet, stood around the anxious Josephine, trying to calm her. Bonaparte finally arrived with his aide-de-camp, Le Marois. It was necessary to wake up Monsieur Le Clercq, who had dozed off. After signing the register, Josephine offered her cheek to be kissed by each person present.

Fortuné had not been consulted. Bonaparte found in the dog a fierce rival, determined to defend his rights and privileges. Fortuné usually slept on his mistress's bed, and when the bridegroom tried to evict him there was a fine rumpus. Josephine did her best to pacify the little creature but finally gave up. Smiling, she told her husband he would have to consent to share the bed with Fortuné or sleep elsewhere. Thus encouraged, the ferocious little pug dog leaped upon the intruder and bit his leg. The general surrendered. A little dog was more formidable than the forty thousand insurgents of the thirteenth of Vendémiaire.

# 2

## Our Lady of Victories

Two days later, General Bonaparte set off toward Nice in a post chaise, with his brother Louis and his aide-de-camp Junot. He went away cheered by Josephine's promise to join him in Italy as soon as he sent for her.

In the weeks that followed she received letter after letter from him, reminding her of her promise and assuring her that all his thoughts were constantly centered upon her. In his imagination he never tired of speculating about what she was doing. "When I imagine you are sad," he wrote, "my heart is torn. When I think of you as gay and amusing yourself with friends, I reproach you for being frivolous, for having no profound emotion, for having forgotten the painful separation so soon. You see, I am not easy to satisfy. . . . Oh, do not be gay, but instead be a little melancholy. . . . Write to me, my dearest, a long letter, and receive the thousand and one kisses I send you. And believe that my love is most tender, most true."

A few days later he was still harping on the same amorous string: "I have not spent one day without loving you; have not spent one night without in imagination pressing you close in my arms. In the midst of urgent affairs, at the head of the troops, while going from camp to camp, my adorable Josephine is alone in my heart, she alone occupies my mind, absorbs all my thoughts."

In letters dated the twenty-third and twenty-sixth of Ventôse [March] Josephine addressed him with the formal pronoun *vous* instead of the intimate *tu*. He immediately wrote back to complain of her lack of warmth, revealing his curiosity and jealousy: "From the twenty-third through the twenty-sixth is four days: What were you doing that you could not write your husband? Oh, my dear! That *vous* and those four days make me regret my former indifference. Cursed be the person who caused it! . . . V*ous!* V*ous!* Ah! What will it be in a fortnight? My soul is sad, my heart is enslaved, and my imagination is frightful! You love me less; one day you will love me no more. . . . I do not ask for eternal love or fidelity, but only *truth*, limitless sincerity. Remember what I have often told you: Nature endowed me with a strong and resolute soul. But she made yours of gauze and lace. Have you ceased loving me? . . ."

Josephine did not talk about her children at all. He knew the reason: it would take too much time to write longer letters. "And your ten-o'clock morning visitors would not have the pleasure of seeing you. . . ." He was annoyed, imploring, accusing, self-accusing, pardoning, in turn: "I receive a letter that you interrupt, you say, to go to the country; and after that, you take on a jealous tone with me, who am overwhelmed here with work and fatigue. Ah, my dearest. . . . It's true that I'm wrong. The country is beautiful in spring; and the nineteen-year-old lover is there, no doubt. How could you be expected to waste an instant writing to one who, separated from you by a distance of three hundred leagues, only lives, feels, exists in the memory of you, and who reads your letters as ravenously as one devours his favorite foods after a six-hour hunt! I am not content. Your last letter is as cold as friendship. I did not find there that fire which lights your glances, and that I sometimes believed I saw. But how capricious I am! I found that your preceding letters oppressed my soul too much. I wanted colder letters, but they give me the icy chill of death. The fear of not being loved by Josephine, the idea of seeing her inconstant, of her. . . . But I forge my punishments . . ."

He announced impending gifts of oranges, of perfume, of orange-blossom cologne, and ended with words of burning tenderness: "A kiss for you, lower, much lower than the breast."

Josephine disliked writing letters. Her apathy and repugnance for the task had already cost her much in Alexandre's distrust and blazing anger. And now Bonaparte was being even more despotic! He expected her to reply to every *one* of his letters! She had foreseen and dreaded his demands, but it was too late now; her tranquillity was shattered. She hated effort, disliked anything sudden and violent, any jolt to her natural indolence. After Bonaparte's departure she had felt free. She could not get used to the idea that he was her husband, much less to his strange Christian name, Napoleon. His frenzies of ardor, his wild transports annoyed her and made her impatient. He was too tormented. In his absence calm had come back to the house on the Rue Chantereine. The calm that follows a Martinique hurricane. Why must he interrupt the slow, comfortable pace of her life?

Josephine had been accused of lacking passion and deep feelings; kind, amiable, and affectionate, yes; but with one aim in life: pleasure and profit. It is true that worldly pleasures attracted her more than the humdrum joys of the hearth; solitude frightened her. She felt helpless against temptations, easily subjugated by smiles and flattering words. And little by little, she took up her old habits, which had been interrupted by a love intrigue she had wished for, but had not foreseen in all its consequences.

The friends whom Bonaparte had kept away now returned to her house. Should she have refused to admit them, renounce their gaiety and humor to please her husband who doubted her fidelity and imagined himself betrayed anyway? Must she turn down invitations to suppers and balls? Wherever fashionable people met, at Saint-Germain-en-Laye, Saint-Cloud, Sèvres, Josephine was the center of attraction, rivaling even her friend Thérésa Tallien. At smart teas, driving in the park, at balls where women dressed most elegantly, her gowns and jewels drew all eyes and made other women pale with envy. And Josephine still reigned with Barras at the Luxembourg Palace and the château of Grosbois, where dark-eyed Madame Hamelin drew gilded swarms of belles and beaux, the *merveilleuses* and the *incroyables*.

Bonaparte, meanwhile, was winning battles for her. In each letter he announced his successes and implored her to join him. Six victories in a fortnight! Piedmont pacified! With each report of victory from the Army of Italy, Josephine received resounding acclamations wherever she went, in the streets, or in her box at the Feydeau Theater. But she could not bring herself to leave Paris and her friends. When friends expressed astonishment and praised her husband enthusiastically, she simply said, "Why, yes, I believe Bonaparte is a worthy man."

Her peaceful existence was disturbed when Napoleon's elder brother, Joseph, appeared at her house with Junot and delivered a letter from the general, insistently demanding that she come to his headquarters at Mondovi:

"If you delay, you will find me ill. The strain and your absence are proving too much. Your letters are my day's pleasure, and my happy days are not frequent." Junot was in Paris, Bonaparte wrote, to deliver twenty-two captured flags. Bonaparte ordered his wife to return to Italy with Junot, whom he could not help envying, for "he will see you, my adorable love, and breathe the air of your temple, while I am alone and far away." He could not wait to have her at his side, "on my heart, in my arms, at my lips." She could not come fast enough for him, but he considered her comfort: "Spread your wings, come, come! But journey by easy stages. The road is hard, long, tiring. . . . Come gently. . . . A kiss on your heart, and then a kiss a little lower, much lower!"

Josephine received Junot and her brother-in-law, whom she was seeing for the first time, very cordially. She asked them about her husband, whom they had seen six days before. She thought Joseph looked very kind. She had heard that his young sister Pauline looked much like him. He had a handsome face with fine, regular features and expressive eyes. Josephine found his manners more agreeable than Bonaparte's or Lucien's. But she was even more attracted to Bonaparte's aide-de-camp, Junot, a fair-haired, blue-eyed young man of twenty-five, whose gentle expression belied his martial bearing and the reports of his daring.

The next day Josephine received another emissary from Bonaparte: Joachim Murat, who brought another long message of imperative tenderness: "Lodgings are prepared for you at Mondovi and at Tortone; from Mondovi you can go to Nice and Genoa: from there visit the rest of Italy, if that will give you pleasure. My happiness is that you be happy, my joy that you be gay, my pleasure that you be pleased. Never was a woman more devotedly loved, or with more passion and tenderness. . . .

"No letter from you. I receive only one every four days, instead of, if you loved me, your writing twice a day. But you must gossip with your little gentlemen who call at ten o'clock in the morning, listen to the nonsense and inanities of a hundred coxcombs until an hour after midnight. In a country of respectable morals everyone is at home by ten o'clock in the evening; and in those countries a woman writes to her husband, thinks about him, lives for him. Adieu, Josephine, you are for me a monster that I can't explain. . . . I love you more each day. Absence cures small passions; it augments the great ones. A kiss on your mouth, on your heart. There is no one but me, *n'est-ce-pas?* And then, one on your breast. How happy Murat is. . . . Ah! if you don't come! . . ."

In this letter he also gave detailed instructions: "Bring your personal maid, and your cook, your coachman; I have carriage

horses here at your service, and a beautiful coach. . . . I wrote
you, by my brother, that there were two hundred gold louis of
mine for your disposition. I am sending two hundred louis by
Murat that you can use for yourself if you have need of them,
or to furnish the apartment you intend to be mine. Only hang
your portrait on all the walls! . . . But, no, the portrait I carry
in my heart is so beautiful that, no matter how beautiful you
are and how clever the painters, you would be lost there. It will
be a very happy day when you cross the Alps. It will be the
most beautiful reward for my pains and the victories I have
accomplished."

Murat was not at all handsome. He had neither the elegant
good looks of the Bonapartes nor Junot's virile grace. But his
curly hair, his strong and rather heavy features, his full lips,
his plumes and bedecked uniform were not at all displeasing
to women. From his attitude and expression, Josephine understood that she could count on him as an ally. She told him she
was in poor health; and since she had said the same only the
night before to her brother-in-law and Junot, who were awaiting Murat's orders, there could be no question of her leaving
immediately. In bad health? Yes, certain discomforts, a kind
of nausea, that women suffer at the beginning of a pregnancy.
In this condition was it wise to undertake such a long and
fatiguing journey? Murat understood what was expected of
him, and undertook to inform his chief of his wife's pregnancy.

While Josephine was rewarding Murat, in her fashion, for
his kindness, she received more moving letters from Bonaparte:

"I am then to be still deprived of the happiness of holding
you in my arms! I am to spend still more months far from
everything I love! Is it possible that I shall not have the happiness of seeing your swollen little body! That must make you
interesting! You write that you are much changed. Your letter
is short, sad, and in a trembling hand. What's the matter, my

adorable one? What can be bothering you? Oh, don't stay in
the country, but in the city where you can find amusement. I
thought I was jealous, but I swear it's not so. ... Know that
my happiness is bound to yours. Soon you will give life to
another human being who will love you as much as I. ... No,
that's not possible, but as much as I will love you. ... I await
Murat with impatience to hear in the greatest detail everything
you are doing, everything you are saying, the people you are
seeing, the clothes you are wearing. Everything that affects
my adored one is dear to my heart ..."

Five days later, the twenty-ninth of Floréal [April], Bonaparte wrote her again from Milan:

"I don't know why, but ever since this morning I am more
content. I have a presentiment that you have started on your
journey. I am dying to see how you look when with child. It
must give you a majestic and respectable air. ... You will make
a pretty little child like its mother, who will love its mother,
who will love you like its father. But till then, see that you
don't love him more than me. I am already beginning to be
jealous. Adieu, *mio dolce amor*, adieu, my well-beloved."

By May Bonaparte was complaining of his loneliness, demanding of Josephine whether she had forgotten him. Why
did she give him no more news? He spoke again of her pregnancy: "Oh, my lovely one, take good care of yourself; be gay,
active, don't worry about anything. ... I constantly imagine
that I see you with your swollen little body; you must be charming; but that unpleasant nausea, do you still have it?"

But he expressed a small doubt in this note, and as time
passed, the doubt became suspicion. Josephine, as Bonaparte
well knew, did not always tell the truth. And the two letters he
wrote her from Milan nineteen days later were despairing,
irritated, and vaguely menacing:

"Josephine, where will you be when this letter reaches you?
If you are in Paris, my unhappiness is certain, you no longer
love me! I can do no more than die. ... Oh! *toi!* ... My tears

are flowing. There is no rest or hope. I respect the will of fate. It crushes me with glory to make me feel my unhappiness more bitterly. I am used to everything about this new state of affairs; but I cannot accustom myself to not esteeming you. No, it's not possible! My Josephine is en route; she loves me at least a little; so much promised love cannot have vanished in two months.

"I detest Paris, women, and love. . . . This is a frightful state. . . . And your conduct. . . . But should I accuse you? No. Your conduct is your destiny. So charming, so beautiful, so sweet, must you be the instrument of my despair? Adieu, my Josephine, the thought of you has made me happy; everything is very much changed. . . . I have reread all your letters tonight, even the one written in your blood. And what feelings they have aroused!"

From tears, Bonaparte passed in his next letter to recriminations, but without bitterness or fury:

"Josephine, you were to have left Paris on the fifth. You were to have left on the eleventh. You had not left on the twelfth. . . . All the couriers arrive without bringing me any letters from you. . . . When you do write, the words are so few, the style never reveals any deep feeling. To love me was a little whim of yours; you already feel how ridiculous it would be to let your heart linger on me. It seems you have made your choice and know to whom you can turn to replace me. I wish you happiness, if inconstancy can give it to you; I will not say perfidy. . . . You have never loved. . . . I had speeded up my military operations; I counted on your being in Milan on the thirteenth, and you are still in Paris. My misfortune is in having known you too little; yours in having judged me by the men who surround you. My heart has never felt anything mediocre. . . . I defended it against love; you inspired it to a boundless passion, an intoxication that degrades it . . .

"Everything pleased me, even the memory of your errors, and the distressing scene that occurred a fortnight before our marriage. Virtue was for me what you did; honor, what pleased you; glory was attractive only because it was agreeable to you and flattered your self-esteem. Your portrait was always in my heart; never a thought without my seeing it and covering it with kisses. But you—you have not looked at my portrait for six months; nothing has escaped me. If I were to go on, I would be loving you without being loved in return, and of all the roles that is the one I cannot play. Josephine, you could have made happy a man less singular than I. You have been, I must tell you, my misfortune. I felt it when my heart was pledged, when every day your heart increased its hold on mine, subjecting all my senses. Cruel one! . . . Why did you raise the hope of a feeling you did not have? Adieu, my happiness, my life, my everything on earth."

While Bonaparte was being tortured by jealousy, Josephine forgot her assumed pregnancy and attended all Madame Tallien's receptions, all the entertainments given by Barras. On the day Junot, now a colonel, brought the captured enemy flags to the Luxembourg Palace and presented them to the Directory, Josephine was standing in the reception line between Madame Récamier and Madame Tallien, her head crowned with flowers. On his way out, Junot, resplendent in the uniform of his new rank, offered one arm to Madame Bonaparte and the other to Madame Tallien, descending the great stairway slowly before a vast crowd. All eyes were upon Josephine and there were cries of "Long live General Bonaparte! Long live Citizeness Bonaparte! Long live Our Lady of the Victories! . . ."

Joseph Bonaparte urged his sister-in-law to leave at once for Italy. Bonaparte no longer believed in her pregnancy. He would believe it even less tomorrow, when he heard of this reception. Joseph reproached her for having let his brother believe, from her latest letter, that she was in danger, that three doctors were constantly at her bedside. And, without pressing the point, he alluded to the all too frequent visits General Murat was paying to the house on the Rue Chantereine.

Josephine protested that she saw Murat very rarely, that she was remaining in Paris simply because the Directory detained her. She promised, however, to make preparations for departure, again set a date . . . and then did not leave.

She loved Paris too much. And there was someone flattering and amusing her, making himself useful in a thousand little ways, whom she could not bring herself to leave behind. It was Hippolyte Charles, a young officer of the Army of Italy, who had quickly made Josephine forget Murat and his rather brusk manners. He was a pleasant, sleek, sturdy, and muscular little man, very dashing in his elegant *hussard's* uniform. Dark-complected and black-haired, he had the hands and feet of a delicate woman; he was witty, a gay companion, a bawdy punster, a merry-maker, a clown, a charming scapegrace . . .

Never had Josephine met a man who understood her so well. His humor and tastes were more suited to her light-hearted and superficial nature than the gravely romantic love of her young husband. The conqueror of Lodi tried in vain to make more legible for his "adorable sovereign" the rapid, impetuous handwriting that made kings tremble. Josephine gave it but an absent-minded glance. Bonaparte's sighs, his complaints and appeals flattered her, but touched her not at all. From the beginning of May to the first days of Messidor [June-July] he received only two letters from her, each of them three lines long. Such indifference tormented him:

"Tell me, you who know how to make others love you without loving them in return, how can one cure one's self of love? I would pay dearly for this remedy. . . . You said you were leaving on the fifth of Prairial; fool that I was, I expected you on the thirteenth. As though a pretty woman could give up her habits, her friends, her Madame Tallien, a dinner with Barras, a performance of a new play, and Fortuné, yes, Fortuné! You love everything more than your husband. You have only a little esteem for him, a little of that kindliness with which your heart abounds."

Josephine smiled as she read those words. It was true. She did cling to her habits, and Bonaparte was not yet a habit. But as she went on reading, her expression became serious, for at the end of the letter, written from Pistoia in Tuscany, Bonaparte became ironical: "You have not written to me; you were ill, you did not come. The Directory did not want you to leave, after your illness; and that little child who was stirring so hard that he hurt you . . ."

Her "little Corsican" saw through her completely. Beneath his mockery, which hurt more than his reproaches, he gave her to understand that he would no longer let himself be fooled. The letter ended with an order:

"You will be at Turin on the tenth; on the twelfth, at Milan, where you will wait for me. . . ." Josephine was overwhelmed by anxiety, and went to Barras for advice. He urged her to leave Paris without delay, and when she still hesitated, he used arguments to frighten her. His own fear dictated his counsel, for Bonaparte had threatened to resign his commission and come to Paris to fetch his wife.

"If you do not leave immediately," Barras said, "Bonaparte will be here before the end of the week."

Josephine wept in despair, as if she were being sent to torture. But the next day, after a farewell supper at the Luxembourg Palace, she set forth in a coach with her dog Fortuné, Joseph Bonaparte, Junot, and her personal maid, Louise Compoint. Hippolyte Charles completed the entourage.

# 3

## *Madame Bonaparte in Milan*

TWO WEEKS LATER, Josephine arrived in Milan. Wild with joy and desire, Bonaparte forgot her silences, her faint show of eagerness, her lies. There followed three days of happiness, three days of passionate embraces, vows, and tears.

An alarming piece of news put an end to this: the Austrian army, headed by General Wurmser, was moving down from the Tyrol to liberate Mantua. Their advance must be checked as quickly as possible. Bonaparte tore himself reluctantly from Josephine's arms and hastened toward Bologna.

Surrounded by the officers stationed in Milan, Madame Bonaparte was received with respect by the greatest families of the city. She lived among endless entertainments and in an intoxicating atmosphere of youth, adulation, glory. She had promised her husband to write often; he continually reminded her of it in his own letters. Even at the most critical hours he did not stop thinking of her, and ceaselessly tormented her with his declarations of passionate love.

While preparing for the siege of Mantua, Bonaparte had visited the village where Virgil was born, stopped on the shores of the lake where the poet had wandered, and in the enchantments of moonlit summer nights he thought only of Josephine.

More and more he asserted his imperious will. When she had barely recovered from the fatigues of the long journey across France and the Alps, he summoned her to Verona, impatient to be with her again. She refused to obey her tyrant, unwilling to be torn away from Milan and complaining of her health. Moreover, he had taken the liberty of opening two letters addressed to "Citizeness Bonaparte," and she was angry. He asked forgiveness, begged for mercy; and grateful for his little surrender, she forgave him.

She had to leave for Brescia, nonetheless, where Bonaparte awaited her. Two days after their reunion, the Austrians appeared before the walls of Mantua, and she was sent back to Milan.

On the return journey she was pursued by an Austrian detachment that fired upon her escort and almost succeeded in capturing her. The cannons of the fortress killed two of her horses, and she was forced to abandon her carriage, leaving in it her silverware and toilet articles, and flee on foot. A peasant offered her his wagon, and she made her humble re-entry into Milan, shivering with fear and enraged at her husband. She was not at all soothed by Bonaparte's letter, declaring that Wurmser would "pay dearly for the tears" he had made her shed.

From Milan she wrote him rarely. Suspicious and worried, Bonaparte went on reporting his triumphs to her—he had overthrown the enemy—but he also complained and raged against her. Overwhelmed with work, grief, and fatigue, must he forswear his conjugal rights because he was far away? "One of these days," he declared, "one of these days a jealous man will crash open your doors, and there I'll be in your arms." Her short letters were to him as glacial "as fifteen years of marriage." Irritated by her lack of passion, which so ill-served his ardor, he scolded her fiercely— and yet at the same time indulgently: "What else can you do that I can complain about? Not love me any more? But that's already done. Hate me? Very well, I wish for it. Everything debases, except hate; indifference with marble pulse, cheating eye, and monotonous step! . . . A thousand, thousand kisses, as tender as my heart."

A harrowing thought struck him, that Josephine might be in the arms of another man while he, himself, was in the thick of battle or dying of a fever. He reproached her for associating with women of questionable reputation like Madame Rugat, who had just frivolously seduced Murat, and Madame Visconti, who had broken the hearts of several young officers. He knew that Josephine had entertained young Caulaincourt in her bedroom "at eleven in the morning—you, who do not get up till one. He had to talk to you about his sister, his mamma. And he had to choose the most convenient hour." Then, in a more menacing tone:

"What then do you do all day, Madame? What important business keeps you from writing to me? . . . Who could this marvelous new lover be who takes up your every minute, the tyrant of your day who prevents you from thinking of your husband?"

She stopped writing to him. She did not even write when he announced his victory at Arcole, where he had narrowly escaped death. She did not respond to his most passionate letters: He longed to hold her in his arms, gaze at her charming body, her slender shoulder, her "soft yet firm little white breasts," and her face "sweet enough to eat," under a Creole kerchief. "You well know," he added, "that I do not forget the 'little visits'; you know, the little dark forest. I send it a thousand kisses and long impatiently to be there again. . . . To live in Josephine is to live in Elysium."

Four months passed. Josephine seemed to have forgotten her lamentable flight from Brescia, and the fact that war was being waged scarcely thirty-five leagues from Milan. At her apartments in the Serbelloni Palace she was treated like a sovereign, receiving presents from the cities of Piedmont and Lombardy, attending receptions, entertainments, and balls in her honor. At the invitation of the Senate of Genoa, she spent four days in that historic city.

On the day set for her return to Milan, she received a letter from Bonaparte. He had returned unexpectedly to Milan, and, not finding her there, accused her of having run away from him, of having abandoned him to "gad about" and attend celebrations: "You no longer care for your dear Napoleon. You loved me as a passing whim; inconstancy has made you indifferent. . . . But I am wrong to demand from you a love like mine. Why expect lace to weigh as much as gold? . . ."

He reassured her with his closing words: "I reopen my letter to give you a kiss. Oh, Josephine, Josephine!" She smiled, sure that she could still make Bonaparte's heart throb, could still, with a word, appease his anger. Away from her, he cursed her; but tomorrow, in her arms, he would be more submissive and tender than ever.

Her departure for Milan, however, was delayed when the wife of the minister of the French Republic at Genoa presented to her a young Parisian painter named Antoine Jean Gros. He was a favorite pupil of the great David, and was to become one of the most fashionable painters of the period. He was then only twenty-five years old, extremely handsome, and a great admirer of Bonaparte, all of which charmed Josephine. When he showed her some of his paintings, and asked to do a portrait of the general, she promised to plead his cause warmly with her husband.

A few days later Gros was dining at the table of the conqueror of Arcole and his wife, whom he looked upon as his fairy godmother. She had rooms prepared for him at the Serbelloni Palace, and Bonaparte agreed to pose for him.

No painter ever had a more impatient, nervous, and hard-to-capture model than Gros had then in Bonaparte. Sometimes, to quiet him, Josephine held him in her arms, the more amusing because of the pose Gros had selected for Bonaparte:

plunging into the thick of battle on the Arcole bridge, bare-headed, hair flowing, resolute unto death, holding a flag.

Two weeks later, Gros finished his portrait to everyone's satisfaction. Bonaparte was so satisfied that he appointed Josephine's protégé to head the committee in charge of searching out the Italian works of art which, by treaty, had been conceded to France.

Marshal Alvinzi, who had been vanquished at Arcole, was attacking anew on the Adige River, while General Provera was trying to disengage Wurmser and the Austrians who were encircled at Mantua. Bonaparte was preparing to leave for Verona when his sister Pauline arrived in Milan.

After Bonaparte's departure, Josephine quickly perceived that she had no friend in Pauline Bonaparte. Flattery, cajolery, kind attentions—nothing Josephine did could break down the hostility of that fantastic and willful girl. Pauline was then sixteen, fresh, pretty, attractive, and soon all the young men were surrounding her. Even Hippolyte Charles made eyes at her. And General Leclerc fell in love.

It was known that Bonaparte was considering giving Pauline in marriage to Leclerc—she herself knew it, but it had no sobering effect upon her naturally high spirits. Encouraged by all the admiration with which she was surrounded, proud of her brother and the affection he had for her, she behaved like a girl newly escaped from convent school, and her whims, her irrepressible gaiety, her turbulent ways soon had the palace in an uproar. Pauline chattered and laughed without rhyme or reason, mockingly imitated the most solemn and dignified, and we are told that she sometimes thrust out her tongue at her sister-in-law's back.

Worse still, Pauline spied upon Josephine and very soon noticed that Hippolyte Charles, now aide-de-camp to General Leclerc, was on extremely good terms with her. It was true: No sooner would Bonaparte leave for a neighboring village than Hippolyte Charles would arrive for lunch at the Serbelloni Palace. Pauline, jealous and indignant, made close inquiries and soon learned that the handsome young cavalier had known Josephine in Paris, had accompanied her not only to Milan but to Genoa, and had even spent two days with her on the shores of Lake Como.

By winks and double talk, Pauline managed to alert Bonaparte. A rather lively scene followed between the commander in chief and his wife and an investigation of Hippolyte Charles was made. It was found that he had engaged in shady transactions with army contractors, and he was arrested. Josephine saved him from the firing squad, but he was discharged from the army and sent back to Paris.

By alternately pouting and humbling herself, Josephine mollified her husband, and at length convinced him that she had been bound to the little officer only by the ties of friendship. Bonaparte forgave, but his doubt remained and was brazenly enjoyed by Pauline: "My sister-in-law nearly died of grief. You don't die of grief at parting from friends. There must have been more there than friendship."

With Charles no longer near, Josephine soon became bored with Milan. Bonaparte's letters no longer burned with the same passion. It was only when he heard that Josephine was sad or ill or wanted to return to Paris that his love was revived. He sent his physician, Dr. Moscati, to her, with a very affectionate letter: "My sweetheart, life is intolerable since I have heard of your sadness. . . . I send you a hundred kisses. Believe me, nothing, unless it be my anxiety, can equal my love."

She did not reply, and her silence made Bonaparte miserable.

"Not a word from you. Good God, what have I done? I think only of you, love only Josephine, live only for my wife, wish only happiness for my dearest, does that make me deserve this harsh treatment? You are ill, or you do not love me! Do you think I have a heart of stone? Do my sufferings affect you so little? I cannot believe it. You to whom nature gave wit, gentleness, beauty, you who alone can reign in my heart, you who doubtless know only too well the absolute hold you have over me! Write to me, think of me, love me."

Out of kindness, and in an effort to persuade her to remain, Bonaparte had her son Eugène brought to Milan. She had been separated from him for eight months, and his arrival seemed to appease her. Now over fifteen, Eugène still had the laughter and frankness of youth, but was acquiring the thoughtfulness of a man. He has been described at this age as "polite without being obsequious, mocking without being impertinent," and throughout his life he was to show great consideration not only for his mother but also for his stepfather.

After the victory of Rivoli, Mantua surrendered in February, 1797, and while the preliminary negotiations for peace were being carried out at Leoben, Bonaparte made a triumphal entry into Milan. A series of receptions followed at the Serbelloni Palace, where Josephine was able to display her talents as an accomplished hostess, a role she played with charm, simplicity, and grace. The palace was too small, now, for the brilliant crowd of aides-de-camp, staff officers, high functionaries of the army, Italian magistrates and their wives, and French émigrés who were dazzled by the genius of the conqueror of Alvinzi, Wurmser, and the Austrian Archduke Charles.

During the negotiations with Austria, Bonaparte established himself at the Mombello Castle, not far from Milan. At this princely residence, he lavishly entertained foreign diplomats and writers. Poets everywhere were celebrating his glory. Josephine was treated by everyone like a queen. And she remembered a prediction an old Negress had made, years before at Trois-Ilets: "You will be queen of France." She was not that yet, but she reigned as queen of Italy.

Bonaparte gathered about him his brothers Joseph and Louis and his sister Pauline. He spoke to Josephine often of the other members of his family, whom he wanted to present to her: his mother Letizia, who was living in Marseilles with her children Elisa, Caroline, and the little Jérôme. Spring was almost at an end when Madame Letizia arrived with her children to meet her brilliant son's wife. She responded with only cold politeness to the embraces of her daughter-in-law, who was not deterred from heaping kind attentions upon her. Josephine was treated no more warmly by her sisters-in-law and her young brother-in-law. Elisa had recently married Captain Bacciochi and Josephine entertained lavishly for the newly wedded pair—but in vain. Pauline's antipathy, and the bad reports made by Joseph and Louis, had had their effect: The Bonapartes were all against her. They considered that in marrying the widow of the Vicomte de Beauharnais, Bonaparte had made a poor match. They regarded Josephine as an intruder, a bothersome and spendthrift adventuress. They told each other she was too old, and repeated the whispers about her personal conduct.

Bonaparte was oblivious to all this, fooled by their pretense of cordiality. And the Bonapartes soon realized that Josephine still exercised too great a sway over her husband to risk showing openly their jealousy and disdain. Elisa, now Madame Bacciochi, was a dried-up, homely young woman, and she sometimes revealed her dislike by rude behavior. Compared to her, Pauline and Caroline behaved charmingly. We can wonder how Josephine saw her husband's relatives, estimating their forces. Caroline was not as perfectly beautiful as Pauline, but she was pretty with a dazzling complexion and exquisite little hands. Jérôme resembled Pauline both in looks and character. Of all the family, the only ones not to engage in secret battle with Josephine were Caroline and Jérôme—both still children—and Joseph's wife, Julie. They alone had no idea of trying to supplant her in Bonaparte's mind and heart.

It must have been with mixed feelings that Josephine arranged the banquets and receptions for the wedding of Pauline and General Leclerc that spring in Milan. But she did not show it, and everything went off smoothly. The wedding feast was followed by an excursion on Lake Como, and when the Leclercs left on their honeymoon, life settled down into a pleasant enough round at Mombello.

Josephine was fond of the flowering gardens and tree-lined paths, and never had Bonaparte been tenderer to her. In the evenings they were surrounded with distinguished guests—military, statesmen, poets. After dinner Bonaparte liked to tell and hear fantastic tales. Then, while Josephine played quiet card games with the ladies—most often *vingt-et-un*—he would sometimes settle down with the men to a game of checkers or "fox and geese" (a game played with dice and counters), taking the games so seriously that he would cheat to win.

A little tragedy for Josephine upset the peaceful life at Mombello. One night, while Fortuné was wandering in the garden he met the cook's dog, a huge mastiff, and challenged him to a fight. The mastiff with one snap of his powerful jaws broke Fortuné's neck. Josephine wept and lamented; nothing could console her except the gift of a new pug dog, who soon proved to be as jealous, arrogant, and bad-tempered as his predecessor.

# 4

## *Pardon*

B<small>Y THE AUTUMN OF</small> 1797 Bonaparte's name was known throughout Europe, from the frontiers he had shifted as a result of the Italian campaign. According to the terms of the treaty concluded at Campo Formio in October, Austria ceded the Belgian provinces to France and recognized the "Cisalpine Republic" that was to be formed in northern Italy. "The little corporal," as his army in Italy had affectionately dubbed him, was still full of plans: a great deal of the world still remained to be conquered. In November, he set off for Rastatt with the King of Prussia, while his family scattered in various directions. Madame Letizia and the Bacciochis returned to Corsica, to put the family house in order. Josephine and Pauline took the road to France, traveling by easy stages.

Shortly after General Bonaparte's return to Paris, the new minister of foreign affairs, Talleyrand, gave a large dinner in honor of the conqueror of Italy. The general wore the embroidered green coat of the French Institute, and Josephine was dressed in a gown of Greek inspiration—yellow, bordered with black—her only jewels, a set of cameos that Pope Pius VII had given her.

In the first rank of the throng that pressed toward him, Bonaparte perceived Madame de Staël, who could not wait to be presented. During the Italian campaign, she had written him several gushing letters. He had not liked their tone, for although she was a friend of Josephine, she spoke of her in tones of contemptuous pity. No doubt, she had written, Josephine was gentle and sweet, but such a woman could never understand the sublime soul of a Bonaparte. She was convinced General Bonaparte and the "daughter of Necker"—her father was the great banker and former minister of finance—were made for each other. A fiery soul such as hers could only have been destined for a hero's adoration. Bonaparte had not even replied to her letters. The impertinence of this female wit, this fabricator of sentiment, daring to compare herself with Josephine!

He thought he had successfully eluded her when suddenly there she was in front of him, her head draped in a turban, a laurel branch in her hand. A circle of curious onlookers gathered at once.

Madame de Staël, after a few complimentary remarks, presented the laurel branch to the conqueror. He refused it.

"Such things must be left to the Muses," he said.

"General," she said, not at all disconcerted, "tell me, what woman do you love most?"

"Mine."

"Obviously. But what kind of woman do you esteem most?"

"The one who knows best how to run her house."

"I concede again. But, come now, which would be first for you among women?"

"The one who bears the most children, Madame."

Piqued and disappointed, she stammered: "They say . . . that you don't like women very much."

"Pardon me, Madame. I love the one I married very much."

Thereupon, he bowed and turned aside, leaving Madame de Staël vexed and irritated at having received such a public affront.

When Bonaparte told Josephine of this conversation, she reproached him for his rudeness—"Parisians will accuse you of talking like a parish priest," she said with a smile. But she was somewhat upset: His replies to Madame de Staël disturbed and wounded her. They seemed to contain a reproach, a cruel allusion to her sterility in her second marriage.

Two months later Bonaparte purchased Josephine's little house on the Rue Chantereine, the street having been renamed, since his return from Italy, the Rue de la Victoire. Josephine soon transformed it, decorating the two reception rooms on the ground floor with gifts received in Italy, and turning the third floor into a study for Bonaparte. On the floor above, she arranged a small drawing room next to a bedroom with twin beds, canopied as if by a tent and ingeniously arranged with a mechanism that could draw them together or apart.

The little house, formerly so tranquil, soon hummed with the voices of scholars, artists, and generals—for the Egyptian campaign was being organized. England would be attacked at her weakest point on the route to India, since Bonaparte had concluded that the Directory's plan of an invasion of the British Isles was impracticable.

There was also a coming and going of Bonapartes. Louis, still too young to be left to himself, sometimes lodged at the house on the Rue de la Victoire, when he did not stay with his brother Joseph in the Rue du Rocher. The Bacciochis had a house on the Rue Verte; Pauline, Madame Leclerc, had taken a house on the Rue Ville-l'Évêque, where Lucien would be accommodated. Caroline was placed in Madame Campan's boarding school at Saint-Germain-en-Laye with Hortense, but they did not become friends, perhaps because Bonaparte had too often vaunted Hortense's virtues, holding her up to Caroline as a model. Indeed, Caroline was not merely jealous of Hortense; she detested her.

Before taking command of the Army of the Orient, Bonaparte married off one of Josephine's nieces, Émilie de Beauharnais, to his aide-de-camp, La Valette. He also had several serious conversations with his elder brother Joseph, and at last all was ready. All plans, for at home as well as abroad, were set and Bonaparte left with Josephine and her son Eugène for Toulon, to take command of the Army of the Orient.

Josephine showed every intention of accompanying her husband and son into Egypt, but her health was bad and the sea voyage, because of English battleships cruising about, was dangerous. Bonaparte rejected the idea, but he promised to send a frigate for her in two months so she could join him. It was understood that she would spend some time at Plombières, in the Vosges region, where the mineral waters from a well called Trou du Capucin were said to have special medicinal value— to revive "languid fecundity."

Josephine's desire to accompany her husband was sincere. She knew that Joseph and Lucien were doing their best to turn him against her, by keeping alive certain suspicions, and she realized that only her presence could dispel any doubts. Moreover, this promised to be a long separation. Bonaparte said he could not estimate how long, perhaps six months—perhaps six years! He had instructed Joseph to set up an annual allowance of 40,000 francs for her.

While her husband and son, with Louis Bonaparte, boarded the *Orient*, Josephine stood at a window of the naval paymaster's building, which overlooked the whole bay, and as the vessels weighed anchor she waved a pathetic farewell. The cannons of the fort and the squadron could not drown out the acclamations of the crowd, the singing of the crews, and the brassy music of the regimental bands. When the *Orient* reached open sea, Josephine shed tears. Bonaparte's departure for Egypt made her not only sad, but gave her a strange feeling that her destiny was about to change . . .

She had no one to turn to but her beloved daughter, and it was to Hortense that she wrote from Toulon: "I am not fatigued by the journey, but very sad at having to leave you so suddenly, without a good-by either to you or my dear Caroline. But I am a little consoled, sweet child, with the hope of embracing you soon. Bonaparte does not want me to embark now. He wants me to take the waters at Plombières before undertaking the voyage to Egypt. He will send for me in two months . . ."

Josephine saw Hortense sooner than she had expected, because of an accident that almost cost her life. One of her friends, a Madame de Cambis, was staying with her at Plombières. One day, as they were standing together on a balcony, it gave way and crashed to the ground. Madame de Cambis broke a leg and Josephine escaped with some bad bruises, but suffered from shock. Hortense was sent for at once and remained with her mother at Plombières for the rest of the stay.

It was there that Josephine first employed a strange man by the name of Carrat, who was soon to dominate not only the other servants but also his mistress. Bold, fawning, greedy, and envious, but not lacking in intelligence, Carrat took the liberty of paying compliments to his mistress and brought her bouquets of flowers daily. He was a droll fellow, with a gift for comic anecdotes, and soon endeared himself to Hortense, who sometimes laughed at his jokes until she cried. When Josephine was on the point of leaving Plombières for Paris, his affliction and grief were so convincing that she consented to take him with her.

In Paris, as personal footman and Madame Bonaparte's hairdresser, Carrat was soon taking all kinds of privileges, being so presumptuous as to scold her for her acts of generosity and particularly for her familiarities with her women servants.

"That's how you ladies are, Madame," he said, "jesting with your domestics! Well, watch out. At the first opportunity, they'll become disrespectful."

Although he objected to her acts of generosity to others, Carrat was not unwilling to benefit from them himself. He put into practice Figaro's words, "Receive, take, ask." And when he wanted something he would say so bluntly: "You ought to give that to me, Madame." Josephine took all this calmly, but she also laughed at the jokes played upon him by the other servants.

Josephine was preparing to leave for Egypt when news reached Paris of the disaster at Abukir. Nelson had destroyed the French fleet there and was now at Naples. Among the vessels seized was the frigate that was to have taken her to the Orient. The fate of her husband and son was uncertain, and she was haunted by fear. It was perhaps an act of courage that she did not discontinue the receptions at her house on the Rue de la Victoire. The Bonapartes stayed away, and, of course, interpreted her conduct otherwise. At this time her most faithful friends were Fanny de Beauharnais, Madame Tallien, Madame Regnault de Saint-Jean-d'Angély, her young and beautiful niece Émilie, now Madame La Valette, the painters Gérard and Girodet, the composer Cherubini, the actor-singer Désaugiers, and the poet Arnault. Arnault had set out with the Egyptian expedition but got no farther than Malta. He found adventure and danger in battle less to his taste than the gossip of drawing rooms and the applause of the public, for whom he had recently written a new heroic tragedy.

In the following spring, Louis Bonaparte returned to France, bearing the flags that had been captured at Malta and Alexandria, and bringing letters to Josephine and Hortense from Bonaparte and Eugène. Louis reassured them that despite the many checks and defeats Bonaparte had conquered Egypt and was now at work reorganizing the country, setting up a new system of law.

Before his departure, Bonaparte had suggested to Josephine that she look for a country estate to purchase. She now looked and found a beautiful old mansion that was particularly desirable because of its nearness to Madame Campan's boarding school in Saint-Germain-en-Laye. After negotiating with the Lecoulteux family who owned it, Josephine acquired the property of Malmaison with a down payment of only 325,000 francs, and immediately moved in.

Malmaison, though pleasantly set in delightful country, was not very conveniently arranged and was in great need of repairs. The park, though cheerful enough, was far from large. A wall surrounded it that extended to the Saint-Germain road, but the lawn in front of the château was not enclosed. One large drawback, which Josephine soon realized and corrected later by acquiring more land, was the nearness of the road. A few short steps and you could see passers-by. Worse still, they could see you.

The Bonapartes were scandalized when they heard of the purchase of Malmaison. Josephine, they declared, had "acquired it as a child buys a doll, without thinking of how long she would like it."

And yet, thanks to the nearness of the river, there was no place so green and flowering as the garden at Malmaison. Nowhere did trees grow as densely with such beautiful, spreading, leafy branches. In a few months General Bonaparte's wife had turned Malmaison into a luxurious residence, with works of art brought back from Italy skillfully placed to adorn the house and gardens. At first there were only a few guests. Hortense came every week or ten days, accompanied by Madame Campan and some of her schoolmates, filling the house with young voices. The girls enjoyed playing pranks, particularly upon Carrat, whose cowardice was equaled only by his fatuousness. He was forever boasting of his successes with women, for the most part imaginary. To hear him talk, no woman had ever been able to resist him, no matter what her station in life.

The girls set out to teach him an unforgettable lesson with Hortense in the lead. They first removed the screws that fastened the slats of his bed and then suspended a jug of water at the head of the bed, which would spill at the least movement. Carrat went to bed in the dark without noticing anything. As Hortense had foreseen, he flung himself heavily down on his bed, which crashed to the floor, while the jug of water spilled all over him. Trembling with anger and fright, and furious at the outburst of laughter in the adjoining room, the poor man shouted, "This is an outrage!" Then, to unnerve him further, Hortense called out very loudly, "Oh, Mamma, the toads and frogs will jump on his face!" And the laughter redoubled.

A Madame de Vergennes, who lived not far from Malmaison, came to call one day, bringing her newly wedded daughter Claire, Madame de Rémusat. Always too trustful and confiding, Josephine, in the course of the conversation, told them things about her husband and brothers-in-law that she could better have kept to herself. Among other things, she said the Bonapartes thought her husband would never return to her, and it was for this reason that they treated her with disdain and neglect. She knew they were circulating gossip about her, knew they were accusing her of always having at her side "a page, a hostler, a cousin, a nephew, at any rate, a young man. . . ." Poor Josephine! How was she to know that young Madame de Rémusat was destined to be one of her most spiteful biographers! She was careful not to mention, however, that while accompanying Hortense to Despréaux's celebrated dancing school, on the Rue du Mont-Blanc, she had met Hippolyte Charles again. The former officer in the *Hussards* poured out his complaints: Bonaparte, by expelling him from the army, had reduced him to humiliating expedients. Josephine, full of pity, recommended him to the Directory and had him made a partner in the food-supplies firm of Bodin, "purveyors to the army." Charles began with a few visits to Malmaison, but soon he was coming every day. Not long after that he was living there—and behaving as though he were the master of the house.

From the road, the inhabitants of the nearby village of Rueil could see the general's wife in a white dress, walking in the garden and leaning on the arm of a young man in a dark coat. They walked slowly in the evening, and by moonlight. They could be seen walking back and forth on the same paths, leaning toward each other. It was a touching sight. Some said that Madame Bonaparte's son had recently returned, and they were talking together about the hero who remained in Egypt.

A year had passed, meanwhile, and Bonaparte had written only a few, very brief letters to his wife. The Allies had pressed forward against the French on all fronts, and were gaining the ascendancy. In France, the Directory was torn with dissension.

Josephine gave two large dinner parties in Paris that year, at which no member of the Bonaparte family was present. Even Louis, who had formerly lived at the house on the Rue de la Victoire, no longer came to pay calls. Of the entire family, only Madame Letizia maintained pleasant relations with Josephine, who had to find allies elsewhere. Josephine set up friendly relations with people in power such as Jean François Rewbell, president of the Directory; Louis Jérôme Gohier, a member of the Directory; and with the political generals Bernadotte, Jourdan, Moulin—all of them enemies of her husband. She cultivated particularly the acquaintance of Gohier, a frenziedly ambitious man who had become president of the Directory after the *coup d'état* of Prairial [June, 1799]. He was a former minister during the Terror, "this casuist of the guillotine," who dreamed of becoming another Washington. He hated Bonaparte, whose increasing popularity upset his personal plans.

The Bonapartes were tirelessly plotting the downfall of Josephine, trying to find some way to induce Bonaparte to divorce her. Joseph and Lucien wrote denunciatory letters to their brother, accusing their sister-in-law and listing her infidelities, pointing to the presence of Hippolyte Charles at Malmaison. Josephine was informed of this by Gohier, and she tried to justify herself. Yes, certainly, she found Hippolyte Charles not unpleasing, but her relations with him remained purely friendly. Gohier was incredulous; appearances were against her. To put an end to suspicion and gossip, she must take a stand, make a choice. As she tearfully resisted, refusing to break off her relations with Charles even though they compromised her, Gohier advised her to divorce Bonaparte. "You must! You tell me that you and Monsieur Charles are nothing more than friends. But if this friendship is so exclusive that it makes you violate the rules of propriety, then I will say, as if there were love between you, divorce Bonaparte. Your 'friendship' sacrifices all other feelings and takes precedence over everything else. And believe me, you will be sorry for all this.

Josephine could not bring herself to take action. Marry Hippolyte Charles? Become Madame Charles, after having been the wife of General Bonaparte? Renounce her honors, descend from the heights to which she had climbed? She could not face such a comedown.

In the spring, there had been the defeat of General Jourdan in the Black Forest, the defeats of General Scherer and General Moreau in Italy, the dissolution of the Congress of Rastatt. These were losses that could not be counterbalanced by the victories of General Bonaparte in far-off Egypt and Syria. When summer brought a series of disasters—the defeat of General Massena at Zurich, of General Macdonald on the Trebbia, and the death of General Joubert at Novi—catastrophe seemed not far off. A frightened Directory summoned General Bonaparte home. But would the summons ever reach him? It was a bare hope. And if the summons did reach him, could he escape Nelson, who now controlled the Mediterranean?

Josephine, while waiting, had Bonaparte's bedroom redecorated. Her strangely casual occupation of wife at a crucial moment is worth mentioning if only to note the originality of her ideas, which established new motifs in furnishings and had an extraordinary influence upon the taste of the times. She had gun carriages of wood painted to look like bronze, and used them as the bases of twin beds. She refurnished Bonaparte's study and the furniture was ornamented with bronze crossed swords. There were little tables in the form and coloring of military drums.

One evening in Vendémiaire [October], when Josephine was dining with her friends the Gohiers, a message was brought in to the president of the Directory toward the end of the meal. After reading and rereading it, he turned to Josephine and said, "Bonaparte is in France." She looked at him gravely. "He landed at Fréjus on the eighteenth. He will be here *Quartidi*,* at the latest."

She interrupted him with a gesture and stood up suddenly. "I shall go to meet him. It is important that I be there before his brothers."

She was preoccupied by one thought: not to lose her position, not to fall from her high estate. She must triumph over Joseph and Lucien now and rejoin her husband before they did, reawaken his love, repossess him.

The next morning she set out in a post chaise without baggage, without even her dog or a servant, taking with her no one but Hortense. They chose the route through Burgundy. Breathless with fear and hope, Josephine kept leaning out of the door to scan the horizon for pursuers. They changed horses at Chalon-sur-Saône where a traveler, recently arrived from Moulins, told them he had seen the general pass by the other route—the Bourbon route.

The news overwhelmed Josephine. It was as if her whole world suddenly crumbled around her. The Bonapartes would take advantage of her absence, and when Bonaparte did not find her at home in the Rue de la Victoire, what would he think? It was clear he would find it an admission of her guilt, her unworthiness of him, and that she had fled from his wrath. The magnitude of the danger gave her courage. She ordered the post chaise to return to Paris. They should be there in

* The fourth day of the Republican calendar's ten-day week.

three days—three days during which the Bonapartes would accuse her, judge her, condemn her. And no one would come to her defense . . .

While the horses galloped along the road, she remained silent and motionless, her eyes staring into the distance, full of despair. Hortense kissed and petted her, saying sweet and encouraging things, but Josephine seemed insensible to her daughter's caresses, seemed to see and hear nothing, and remained sunk in the contemplation of her misfortune.

She was thirty-seven years old, not an age to start a new life descended from such a height. If Bonaparte refused to hear her, if he showed lack of feeling, what would she do? Where could she go without money or credit, dragging her debts after her? She owed everyone—more than a million to her tradesmen. Only the house at Malmaison was paid for, and she owed 300,000 francs for the estate. Credulous, spendthrift, unreasonable in her desires, and at the mercy of her whims, she had let herself be cheated by merchants of dubious character. In the department of Dyle [now a part of Belgium] she had bought national property without seeing it— Who whould pay those 1,300,000 francs? Madame Renaudin, who had recently married her old lover and was now the Marquise de Beauharnais, had pledged herself for a third of the sum; but she, alas, was much less rich in money than in promises.

Where would she live? The house on the Rue de la Victoire belonged to Bonaparte. She had accumulated masses of pearls, diamonds, and cameos at Malmaison—with what pride she had shown them to her friends; and there were also at Malmaison statues and paintings, the countless objects of art that were her Italian spoils. Could she realize enough from their sale to satisfy her creditors?

Her thoughts moved further afield toward her children who would share her distress. She loved them both tenderly. What would become of them—of Eugène, whom Bonaparte treated like a son and whose future he proposed to assure? And her sweet Hortense beside her, so good and so affectionate? Who would want to marry her?

Wherever they stopped, people crowded round their carriage, cheering and shouting. Was it true, they asked, that their "savior" had at last returned?

The "savior" had just arrived in Paris, with Eugène. It was six o'clock in the morning when his carriage stopped in front of the little house on the Rue de la Victoire. His mother was waiting for him there, with all her family. When he didn't see his wife, Bonaparte looked very disturbed and demanded to know why she was not there. Was she ill? Madame Letizia shook her head significantly. Elisa and Pauline exchanged meaningful smiles. Joseph's eyes were full of compassion. Lucien made a sympathetic gesture with his hand. Bonaparte turned pale. "Has she...." He frowned and finished the question silently: Had Josephine, fearing his vengeance, run off with the craven Hippolyte Charles?

When he entered the house forsaken by its mistress, everything reminded him of their love and he was momentarily overwhelmed by his former tenderness. Then, once more, he exploded in shouts of grief and rage. He resolved never again to see his wife who had treated his feelings so lightly. He would never take her back. There could be nothing more between them.

A friend followed him to his bedroom where he crouched by the fireplace, furiously stirring the fire. The friend was the financier Collot, who had negotiated the contracts for the supplies of the Army of Italy and rendered many personal services of a financial nature. Collot did not forget the help Josephine had given him, and he in no way shared the Bonapartes' opinion of her.

"What, General!" he exclaimed. "You intend to repudiate your wife?"

"Isn't that what she deserves?" shouted Bonaparte, straightening up.

"I am not qualified to speak on that subject. But is this the moment to worry about it? Think, instead, of France. The people of France have their eyes upon you. They expect you to devote all your time to their welfare. If they see you in the midst of domestic squabbles, your grandeur will vanish. You will become just one more husband, foolishly betrayed by his wife in the Molière fashion. Forget your grievances toward your wife and turn your attention to the State, which needs your assistance ..."

"No!" shouted Bonaparte. "I must finish with her. She will never again set foot in my house. I'm not concerned with what people say. They will gossip about us for a day or two, and on the third day they'll forget it. In the midst of mounting events what does a broken marriage matter? My troubles would not even be noticed ..."

The financier continued to plead with him to behave with restraint and gentleness.

"Very well," Bonaparte said at length. "My wife shall go to Malmaison. But, as for me, I'll remain here. The public knows enough not to be fooled about the reason for our separation."

"Your violent attitude," Collot quietly said, "proves that you still love her. She will arrive and excuse herself. You will pardon her and become calmer."

"*Pardon* her?" Bonaparte interrupted. And in a hard voice, his hands clenched on his chest, he said chokingly, "Pardon her? Never, never! I would rather tear out my heart and throw it on the fire."

At the beginning of the scene, Eugène had withdrawn to his room on the top floor. Crushed with grief, he recalled what had happened three months before in Egypt, when Bonaparte had received letters from Josephine's enemies, chiefly Lucien. He remembered vividly the intimate confessions Bonaparte had made to him. Despite his youth, Eugène inspired sufficient trust for the general to pour out his heart freely to him. It was usually in the evenings that the general poured out his grief, striding up and down in his tent. Eugène had always tried to pacify him and offset the effect of Lucien's letters. He consoled him as best he could, considering his youth and the respect in which he held the general.

Eugène refused to judge his mother. Torn and tormented by the fear of ceasing to love and respect her, he refused to believe in her guilt.

Two days later, at eleven o'clock in the evening, Eugène heard loud cries, and shortly afterward the chambermaid came to announce the arrival of Hortense and Josephine. She reported that Bonaparte had shut himself in his study and refused to respond to his wife's appeals.

Eugène ran downstairs and found his mother and sister outside the study door. Josephine was weeping, and in a voice choked with heart-rending sobs implored her husband:

"Let me in, my dearest, my heart's dearest," she was saying. "Open the door. I will tell you everything, explain everything . . ."

She went on talking and weeping, pleading, searching for the sweetest words to sway him. For hours she carried on like this, gently knocking at the door, weeping and calling out to her husband in turn. But the door remained shut. Finally, in despair and at the end of her strength, she fell upon her knees, shaken by a nervous trembling.

The good chambermaid pitied and tried to soothe her. Eugène and Hortense wept. Suddenly, Josephine seemed to recover new strength. She heard a noise in the room, a footstep, *his* footstep. She started up, then again fell inert, intently listening. The key creaked in the lock, the door slowly opened, and Bonaparte appeared, his face white, contorted with suffering, his eyes reddened with tears. Josephine looked at him fixedly, dazed and bewildered, and stayed on her knees. Then slowly she held out her arms to him, stammering meaningless words in a low voice, overwhelmed, panting with fear.

Bonaparte talked as if no one else but she were there; as though he could not see Eugène, Hortense, and the maid standing motionless beside her. He poured out his heart to her, put into words his suspicions, his struggles and revulsions against them, his efforts not to believe the accusing letters he had received in Egypt; his despair, his fury, his thoughts of vengeance; the entire, long, humiliating torture he had undergone in the past few months. . . . He ended by announcing an eternal separation . . .

Josephine replied with gentle words, protesting her innocence, justifying herself, accusing her sisters- and brothers-in-law of detesting her, asserting they would do anything in their power to destroy her. Eugène and Hortense mingled their pleas with hers. At the sound of their voices Bonaparte started, and only then became aware of their presence. He weakened visibly, his voice less harsh, his words less bitter.

After a heart-rending scene of mingled reproaches, indignant protestations, promises, cries, sobs, and prayers, Bonaparte lifted his wife from her knees. Exhausted by her tears and her grief-stricken efforts to be brave, Josephine collapsed in his arms, sure of his unreserving pardon.

# 5

## *Josephine in the Palace of Kings*

ONE EVENING, about a month after Bonaparte's return from Egypt, the rumor spread that a traitorous attempt on his life had been made at Saint-Cloud. The Rue de la Victoire was jammed with pedestrians, horses, and carriages, and the air was filled with shouts and dispute, exclamations and curses, as horsemen galloped up, "knocking down everything in their way," and entered the courtyard of General Bonaparte's town house. The crowd increased their shouting to a deafening uproar.

Josephine waited anxiously for news in her bedroom. She knew that a *coup d'état* had been prepared, that the transfer to Saint-Cloud of the two legislative assemblies was a provocation. Only the night before she had witnessed a stormy meeting between Bonaparte and Botot, Barras's secretary.

"What have you done with this France that I left with you in such good condition?" Bonaparte had thundered. "I left you peace, I find war! I left you victories, I find defeats."

This placed the blame squarely upon the Directory and called upon the executive arm of the government to account for the country's plight. Torn by strife between the Jacobins and the Moderates, weakened by the defeats of her armies in Italy and on the Rhine, ruined by the malpractices of government heads, and despoiled by army contractors, the Republic was in the throes of agony. A stronger executive power was needed to pull her out of it, thought Bonaparte, as did his brother Lucien and the Abbé Sieyès, who had replaced Rewbell in the Directory and drawn up and submitted a new constitution to the assemblies.

The vote was to be taken at Saint-Cloud today. What had happened?

Josephine's uncertainty lasted until late that night when Fouché, the recently appointed minister of police, arrived at the house to announce: "All is well." Bonaparte, while addressing the Council of Five Hundred, had been jostled by some Jacobin deputies who had shouted, "Down with the dictator! Down with the tyrant! Outlaw him!" Grenadiers had pitched into the mêlée and torn the general away from his assailants. When he reappeared, his face, which had been slightly scratched during the disturbance, was bleeding. Hence the rumor of an attempt on his life.

Fouché talked for some time with Josephine, recounting the events in a calm voice. "The tumult increased," he said. "Then Lucien, who was presiding, threw off his gown and left the Assembly to rejoin Bonaparte. Afterward, they both harangued the troops. There was a beating of drums, a battalion of grenadiers marched up. Murat, taking command of them, invaded the Chamber and drove out the deputies—who fled into the woods." Lucien had gathered together those who remained and this residue of the Five Hundred had approved the new constitution by vote. Provision was made for government by three consuls instead of five directors, and Bonaparte, Sieyès, and Roger Ducos were elected.

"Madame, you may now sleep peacefully," concluded Fouché. "Everything has happened for the best."

Bonaparte came home about four o'clock in the morning with his personal secretary, Bourrienne. Josephine was sitting up with Madame Letizia and Pauline, waiting for him. They discussed the danger he had faced in the Assembly; but he was already thinking about the following day and the work that lay ahead.

"Without us, the country was lost," said Bonaparte suddenly, addressing himself to Bourrienne. "The Jacobins will grumble and accuse, but we will proudly reply, as did a certain Roman: 'We have saved our country; now let us render thanks to the gods.'"

A month later, Bonaparte became First Consul. His term was to last ten years, during which Sieyès and Roger Ducos were replaced by two more easily managed men, Cambacérès and Lebrun.

The new government was installed in the Luxembourg.

Bonaparte seemed to have forgotten all Josephine's faults. She had cleverly aided him in the preparation of the *coup d'état* of the eighteenth of Brumaire, by flattering those who hesitated, scheming with Barras, pulling the wool over Gohier's eyes, and generally lulling suspicion. Bonaparte seemed to have forgotten her weaknesses, but she felt strongly that he did not love her as before. He no longer thought of divorce, no longer threatened her with it as he had often done right after his return from Egypt. But there was nothing between them now except that "tenderness of habit and that intimate harmony" which make a marriage last. She realized that she would have to devote herself entirely to her husband if their reconciliation was to be more than an empty word. She must give the Bonaparte family no cause for hostility since they, of course, had not forgiven her. She must make them her allies; put an end to their hatred. She considered the possibility of marrying Hortense to one of Bonaparte's brothers.

Jérôme was fifteen, a year younger than Hortense. Attracted by the fair hair and blue eyes of his "pretty half-sister," as he called her, Jérôme often came to the house on the Rue de la Victoire. The two young people saw a great deal of each other, Josephine encouraged their friendship and often left them alone. When the Bonapartes became aware of her plans, they did all they could to frustrate them. Jérôme continued to visit the house, to stroll in the garden with Hortense, but he was careful not to entertain the idea of falling in love.

At about this same time—early in the year 1800—Caroline Bonaparte married General Murat. The marriage contract was signed at the Luxembourg Palace, and the wedding took place in Mortefontaine, at the home of Joseph Bonaparte.

Josephine had an apartment on the first floor of the Petit-Luxembourg, where in the evenings she received a few close friends and their wives: the Second Consul Cambacérès, Monsieur de Talleyrand, and the ministers Berthier, Fouché, Gaudin, and Laplace. It was in her *salon* that the form of address "Madame" was restored to politeness, replacing the Republican "Citizeness." Her little drawing room was also filled every morning with royalist *émigrés*, who had returned to France thanks to Josephine's pleas to Bonaparte in their behalf.

To restore to activity the Lyons silk factories, the First Consul forbade the wearing of materials manufactured in England. If he noticed Josephine or Hortense wearing new dresses, he would ask curtly: "Is that French material?" Josephine would make some such reply as, "Yes, it's Saint-Quentin lawn." But if her smile betrayed a lie, Bonaparte would tear the fragile dress to shreds. He was determined that everyone should wear only French satins and velvets, and it became a dictate of fashion. Soon no item of dress except cashmere shawls survived the taboo on foreign goods.

The First Consul considered himself badly accommodated at the Luxembourg, and a few months after settling there, he decided it was time to make a change. He announced the proposed move to his secretary Bourrienne, on the thirtieth of Pluviôse, in the presence of Josephine. It is reported that he said, "Tonight we'll sleep at the Tuileries," and that, while speaking, he pinched and kissed his wife.

At the Tuileries, the palace of the kings of France, Josephine was given the respectful attentions befitting a queen, but she could not shake off a feeling of great sadness. "I shall not be happy here," she remarked to her daughter. "I have gloomy forebodings."

In the royal apartments, which had stood empty since August 10, 1792, the plaintive ghost of Marie Antoinette seemed to wander. When Hortense announced her desire to return to Madame Campan's school Josephine wept and reproached her daughter. The First Consul caught them in such a scene, with Josephine tearfully accusing Hortense of preferring her friends to her mother.

"So you think," said the First Consul, laughing, "that you made your children for yourself alone? Try to realize that when they grow up, children do not need their parents. And the day your daughter marries, you will be nothing more to her . . ."

Hortense interrupted with a vigorous denial. But Bonaparte blithely ignored her. "Children always love their parents less in return than they are loved. It's only natural. Look at nestlings: As soon as they can fly, they are off never to come back."

Josephine burst into tears. He took her in his arms, kissed her, and soothed her, while explaining in a half-mocking, half-serious tone, "Oh, the poor little woman! How unhappy she is! She has a husband who loves only her, and that's not enough. I'm the one who should be angry: You love your children more than you love me."

Josephine shook her head. No, Bonaparte must never doubt her attachment for him. But to be absolutely happy she must have her children nearby.

"What do you lack for happiness?" the First Consul asked. "You have a husband who is certainly as good as any, and two children who adore you. Come, you were born lucky, weren't you?"

She laughed through her tears, and her gaiety returned. But Hortense realized she must never mention Saint-Germain again. She was given two rooms adjoining her mother's dressing room, in one of which she slept. In the other room she painted, although it was not big enough for an artist's studio, and was soon almost unendurable from the odor of turpentine.

Situated on the ground floor of the palace, between the Pavillon de l'Horloge and the Pavillon de Flore, Josephine's suite of rooms opened out on the garden. She had it decorated in excellent taste, but not luxuriously. The large drawing-room walls were covered with silk in a shade of yellow known as Quinze-Seize, and the furniture was mahogany. The upholsterings and hangings were of an Indian silk stuff—known as *gourgouran*—with silk, but not gold, fringes. Everything in all her rooms was simple, elegant, and fresh.

Josephine entertained her intimate friends and received morning visitors in her own rooms. The large receptions took place on the floor above, where the First Consul had his apartments. When his work was over for the day, Bonaparte would go down to his wife by a narrow little dark stairway, "which opened out of a clothes closet adjoining his study."

Every morning, the Marquis de Caulaincourt called on Madame Bonaparte. He arrived at the Tuileries mounted on a pony that was adorned with a velvet saddle and a golden snaffle. Other friends, who had been faithful visitors at Josephine's little house on the Rue Chantereine, and after, when the house became Bonaparte's and the street became the Rue de la Victoire, called on her regularly, among them the Marquis de Ségur and his son, and the Vicomte de Noailles.

At night, the Bonapartes often entertained their intimate friends in the Yellow Drawing Room, lighted by clusters of candles that were shaded with gauze to soften their light. At these small receptions, Josephine usually sat by the fireplace working at her tapestry frame, but it is said that the tapestry, at least "three quarters of it," came from the hands of Mademoiselle Dubuquoy, one of Josephine's ladies in waiting. Mademoiselle Dubuquoy had stimulated Josephine's interest

in the occupation by saying how clever Marie Antoinette had
been at such hand work. The needlework enabled Josephine to
listen, rather than talk, when the subject turned on something
beyond her interest. Then she preferred to listen to her daughter or husband. Hortense usually sat on the other side of the
fireplace from her mother, always graceful and gay, and charming everyone. Bonaparte usually remained standing with his
back to the fire, relaxed but talking vivaciously, sometimes
interrupting himself to stir the fire or take a lightning-quick
pinch of snuff.

Every ten days the First Consul gave a dinner for more than
a hundred guests in the Gallery of Diana. Despite the protests
and tears of his wife, Bonaparte excluded from these receptions most of her old friends. Shabby noblemen, new-rich
tradesmen, gentlemen-gamblers on the stock exchange, and
cynical old fops gradually disappeared from the scene. No
longer were divorced women or women of doubtful virtue admitted to the Tuileries. Madame Tallien disappeared along
with the ugly but charming Madame Hamelin. Tallien had
been captured by a British cruiser in the Mediterranean, and
was now in England, while his wife stayed in Paris and was often
seen in public places with a rich banker, Monsieur Ouvrard.
Monsieur and Madame Gohier also no longer attended Josephine's parties, for Gohier had retired from the political scene
following the Brumaire *coup d'état*.

But gentlemen of the old nobility such as Caulaincourt,
Mun, Ségur, and Noailles were there with their wives, most
of whom were young and pretty. There were many pretty
women at the Tuileries receptions but perhaps none were
more admired than the First Consul's sister Caroline, now
Madame Murat, and Josephine's niece, Émilie de Beauharnais,
now Madame de La Valette. Madame de Rémusat was usually
present, along with Madame de la Rochefoucauld, who was
much admired and liked for her wit, and Madame Laplace,

wife of the great mathematician and astronomer, who, it was said, "did everything geometrically—even her curtsies—to please her husband."

In short, an elegant new, and very select, society was gradually forming around the First Consul and his wife.

# 6

## The Marriage of Hortense

WITH CONFIDENCE and order returning, political differ-
ences were gradually settled. Aristocrats who had left
France during the Terror and dissidents who had been banished into exile by the Directory came back. The people of
France, delighted with the restoration of peace and calm, set
to work again, and the country prospered.

In the meantime, the Austrians, emboldened by Bonaparte's absence from the front, again invaded Italy, besieged
Genoa, and threatened Provence. The First Consul crossed
the Alps. One month later, in June, all France acclaimed the
conqueror of Marengo.

Upon his return to the Tuileries, the First Consul established new habits. He no longer kept fixed hours for his meals
and sleep. He lunched alone and hurriedly. Josephine and
Hortense saw nothing of him until dinnertime. Occasionally
he came downstairs earlier than usual and would enter his
wife's dressing room. If he found Josephine still dressing, he
would rumple her hair, rearrange the flowers in it to his own
liking, and declare, very seriously, that they looked much better that way.

Bonaparte was preoccupied, Josephine knew that she must
not disturb his train of thought. While waiting for dinner, he
sat by the fireplace with a pensive air, or walked up and down

the room, addressing Josephine's maid curtly with "Not ready yet?" He remained silent throughout dinner, which lasted ten minutes, and more often than not left the table before the end of the meal. When Josephine remarked on it, he would smile and sit down again, but then almost at once would depart without having spoken a word to anyone.

The victory of Marengo and, a few months later, the victory of Hohenlinden, won by General Moreau, allowed a number of young army officers both on the Rhine and in Italy to return to France. Many of them were married. Josephine received their young wives with such gracious kindness that she put them immediately at ease. Her circle of friends was thus increased. She was especially fond of Madame Lannes, the wife of General Lannes (who was later to be made the Duc de Montebello), of Madame Savary, wife of General Savary (later Duc de Rovigo), and Madame Mortier, wife of General Mortier (later Duc de Trévise). They were pretty young women, gay and prepossessing, and they were distinguished.

Josephine immediately took a liking to Laure Junot, the well-born wife of Napoleon's former aide-de-camp and secretary, Andoche Junot, who was now general of a brigade in Egypt and was later to become Duc d'Abrantès; it was under the name of the Duchesse d'Abrantès that Laure Junot wrote her memoirs, which, alas, are more than spiteful.

Josephine had a useful friend in the wife of General Marmont (later Duc de Raguse), who was the daughter of the wealthy banker, Perregaux. Some of these women were only slightly older than Hortense, among them was Madame Ney, who was the wife of Michel Ney (later Duc d'Elchingen), then just beginning a career that was to be both glorious and tragic. Madame Ney was a niece of Madame Campan, and had been a schoolmate and friend of Hortense.

Taking advantage of Bonaparte's policy of reconciling all parties, the wives of *émigrés* who returned to France at this time sought to win over Josephine to the royalist cause. Knowing her sympathies for the old nobility and her influence over the First Consul, they offered tempting rewards, promising Bonaparte the command of the royal armies if Louis XVIII were restored to the throne. And indeed, when Louis XVIII wrote to Bonaparte from Mittau, demanding the restoration of the throne to the Bourbons, Josephine implored her husband not to refuse, at least not too categorically.

"You are insane!" said Bonaparte, who had first smiled at the idea, but frowned when Hortense took sides with her mother. "Insane! The society of the Faubourg Saint-Germain has turned your heads."

That very day he wrote a reply to the exiled King: "Surely you do not want to return to France," he argued with the royal pretender, "for it would mean that you would have to march over a hundred thousand corpses. . . . I am not insensible to the misfortunes of your family, however, and will contribute with pleasure to the comfort and tranquillity of your life in retirement."

Other attempts at overthrowing the government of the First Consul met with the same rebuffs, but both royalists and Jacobins continued their plotting, and toward the end of the year there was such restlessness that Bonaparte's life was often in danger.

On the third of Nivôse, he narrowly escaped being assassinated, whether as a result of Jacobin or royalist plots is still a matter of debate. That night there was to be a performance of the new cantata by Haydn, *Creation*. Bonaparte sat by the fire and refused to go. Josephine was insistent. "Do go," she urged. "It will be a diversion. You work too hard." The First Consul finally let himself be persuaded.

As Bonaparte got into his carriage, he criticized the way Josephine had draped her shawl, and she asked Colonel Rapp, the aide-de-camp, to arrange it in the Egyptian fashion. While her shawl was being rearranged, the carriage of the First Consul had driven on ahead, so that Josephine's carriage was separated from it by some distance. They had almost reached the theater when a loud explosion made her carriage tremble. The window glass shattered, slightly wounding Hortense. The horses, suffocated by the smell of explosives, took fright and bolted. Josephine stammered, "It's against Bonaparte . . ." and fainted in Hortense's arms.

She could not hold back her tears when she saw the First Consul in his box, being acclaimed by two thousand frenzied spectators. Calm and smiling, as if the criminal attempt had not been directed at him, he tried to soothe Josephine. "What's wrong? What happened?" he asked her. "Why, it's nothing." But she continued to shudder with fear and stared fixedly at her husband.

The next day Bonaparte summoned Fouché, reprimanded him for his carelessness, and accused the Jacobins of having been the authors of the plot. The minister of police protested, saying that the royalists were the guilty ones. Bonaparte, who had consulted with Pierre Louis Roederer, a politician and economist whose advice he was learning to value, firmly asserted that Fouché had been careless in setting up safeguards against the "Jacobin terrorists." Talleyrand advised him to arrest and shoot the minister of police.

When Josephine heard of this she sided with Fouché against his detractors. "She's defending her own interests," declared the Bonaparte family. Did she not receive from Fouché a percentage of the income from gambling houses? They specified the amount: one thousand francs a day. They said that Fouché paid her to keep him informed of what went on at the Tuileries. According to Lucien, this money was transmitted to her by Madame de Copons, the widow of a magistrate and in some way related to Josephine. Lucien hated Josephine so much he fearlessly spread these defamatory rumors which made out his sister-in-law to be one of Fouché's chief spies. How, otherwise, said he, could Josephine's extravagance, her constant spending, her luxuries be explained? This was willful misrepresentation, of course, for Lucien knew that Bonaparte had paid off his wife's debts. He, who detested waste, had paid the 1,200,000 francs his wife owed to various tradesmen, had paid the notes of the upholsterer, saddle maker, carriage builder, and dressmakers.

But it was true that Josephine could not stop spending. Beautiful fabrics, delicate flowers, jewels, laces, bibelots, anything and everything costly and rare attracted her. Lucien still recalled a strange, white crepe dress she had worn one day when he received her at his country home at Plessis-Chamant, near Senlis. Toucan feathers were sewed all over it, and gleaming at the tip of each feather was a seed pearl. In her hair, which had been dressed by the most elegant hairdresser Duplan, she had arranged garlands of toucan feathers mingled with pearls. Her jewels, that day, were a complete set of rubies!

A Lucien who was so severe with an assuredly coquettish woman, was more indulgent with himself. As minister of the interior he had acquired wealth in shady speculations and had bought and furnished the Plessis-Chamant château at great expense. His elaborate receptions, his gambling, his expenditures on his mistresses were a source of irritation to the First Consul. Lucien's ambition, swollen by that of Joseph, had inspired him to publish a pamphlet, in which Madame Bonaparte could easily read an exhortation to divorce. This brochure, entitled *Parallel between Caesar, Cromwell, and Bonaparte*, put rather brutally the question: "Where are Bonaparte's heirs?" Moved by his wife's complaints, and alarmed at the dangerous ambitions of his brothers, Bonaparte saw "a personal challenge" in this pamphlet. Lucien was repudiated and disgraced and sent as ambassador to the court of Madrid.

It was largely to revenge himself upon his sister-in-law that most of Lucien's ambitious schemes in Spain were carried out, none more outrageous than his negotiations for the marriage of the Infanta Isabella and Bonaparte. The First Consul did not reply to these offers, but he did inform Josephine of them. She was overwhelmed, but he reassured her: No intrigue could separate them from each other. Many months later, upon seeing Lucien again, Bonaparte alluded to the Infanta of Spain, remarking that, with a little more provocation, Josephine would have become Lucien's mortal enemy. "But of course," he added, "she is as devoid of venom as a pigeon."

"Why did you tell her?" asked Lucien. "She would, quite naturally, be aggrieved."

The question must have occurred to Josephine herself many times in the subsequent months. She was aggrieved at the thought that her sterility was becoming a question of State, no matter who was responsible—she or Bonaparte.

Bonaparte often jested about it in front of his brothers and sisters. Perhaps he was not capable of perpetuating his race? The mistresses he had had in Egypt and more recently in Italy had borne him no children. Bonaparte's sisters always scoffed at the idea that he was incapable of procreation. They preferred to blame Josephine, and their talk was not calculated to calm her terror of divorce. "You forget," she said to them one day, "that I had children by my first husband." "True," countered Elisa, "but you were younger then."

This impulsive remark of Madame Bacciochi was a measure to Josephine of the hatred the Bonapartes had for her, and her eyes filled with tears.

"Now what's the matter?" asked Bonaparte, who just then arrived on the scene. "Why are you crying?" When he heard the reason he scolded his sister for her "imprudence," and concluded with, "You ought to know it's not good to tell the whole truth."

Far from appeasing Josephine, these words only added to her grief. Even Lucien was struck with pity. "Come," he said to her in a low voice, "come, my sister, prove to the Consul that he is mistaken, and quickly give us a little Caesar."

A Dr. Corvisart was called in for consultation, who prescribed the waters at Plombières, even though Josephine had already spent a season there without results. She obediently went off again, accompanied by Hortense and Madame Letizia.

The First Consul's letters to Josephine at Plombières, that year, were dry and brief, very different from those he had written her five years before. They merely give the news, and seem laboriously written: "The weather is so bad that I have stayed in Paris. It's too dreary at Malmaison without you.... The medical blister the doctor put on my arm is very painful. I received from London some plants for you, and have sent them to your gardener. If the weather is as bad at Plombières as it is here, you will suffer a great deal from the waters! Many kind regards to Mamma and Hortense."

Hortense was now eighteen and seductively beautiful with her fine complexion, lovely eyes, lithe figure, and beautiful hands and arms—almost a blue-eyed replica of Josephine at the same age. Even her character and accomplishments resembled those of her mother, for she was gracious and sweet, though not lacking wit and malice. She danced delightfully, and thanks to art lessons with Isabey, she painted very well. Her mother was now urging her to marry soon, saying she was "too old" to wait. Josephine recalled that at only a slightly more advanced age she had already borne her two children.

But Hortense wanted to marry only a man she loved. She had had a number of suitors and had rejected them all. Rewbell's son was one of them; another, the son of the wealthy Mun who, though rich and charming, was too close a friend of Madame de Staël to suit her. There had been several offers from titled families as well—the Comte de Gontaut, the Comte de Noailles, among others.

Upon her return to Paris Josephine redoubled her efforts to marry Hortense off to a member of the Bonaparte family. By giving them her daughter, she hoped to disarm her worst enemies, to be able to live at peace with them, and with the specter of divorce banished forever. She considered Lucien first of all. He was now a widower, twenty-seven years old, and while in Madrid had managed to make a fortune. But Lucien declined her offers. He had no intention of remarrying, he said. He dared not confess that he had a mistress, the divorced wife of a certain Jouberthon, whom he had met at a gay party of his friends, the Labordes. Josephine next aimed at Louis Bonaparte.

But Hortense was in love with General Duroc, onetime aide-de-camp of Bonaparte and now grand marshal of the Tuileries. The First Consul was inclined to favor the match, knowing Duroc was wholly devoted to him. But Josephine opposed this union because it upset her plans. Moreover, "I could never get used to hearing you called Madame Duroc," she told Hortense! The First Consul was obdurate and, to change his mind, Josephine had to use persuasion, tears, prayers, and artful flatteries. With Duroc out of the way, she again suggested Louis. Hortense felt an aversion to him, but held out for only a week before yielding. Louis made no objection.

The wedding was celebrated at the Tuileries on a June evening in 1802, with the mayor of the first *arrondissement* officiating. Late that night the religious rites were performed by Cardinal Caprara at the house on the Rue de la Victoire, where the big drawing room on the ground floor had been transformed into a chapel for the occasion.

This ceremony was in fact a double wedding and might have been a triple wedding, if Josephine had had her way. For, two years before, Caroline Bonaparte had married Joachim Murat only in a civil ceremony and they took this occasion to have their union consecrated by the Church. Josephine and Bonaparte had likewise been married without the blessing of the Church, and she had wept and implored her husband to have their marriage celebrated according to the rites of the Church by Cardinal Caprara. Bonaparte refused to comply and Josephine, always insecure, could not doubt that he wished to be able to break up their marriage at his convenience.

Louis—contemptuous, hard, capricious, mistrustful, over-sensitive, embittered, and suffering from a disease contracted in Egypt—soon proved to be insupportable. A week before his marriage, Lucien had advised him not to be taken in by the charms of the lovely Hortense, to remember that his happiness, liberty, and above all his honor were at stake. At the time, believing himself to be in love, Louis preferred to disregard his brother's advice. But soon afterward Lucien's words came back to him and were transformed into suspicions by his sick mind.

One day, during a violent quarrel, he spoke out in a surprising way for one usually so taciturn. He intended to enlighten Hortense "on all the failings attributed to her mother," and gave a detailed account of the gossip about Josephine, declaring he wanted to avoid the fate common to husbands and demanding that Hortense stop all contact with such a mother! From now on, he reminded Hortense, she belonged to the Bonaparte family. "Our interests should be yours," he said. "The interests of your own family no longer concern you."

Other quarrels followed, arising over trifles or brought on by Louis's imagination. His easily wounded self-esteem, jealousy, and instability flamed into a persecution complex, sometimes to the heat of delirium.

The First Consul reproached his brother severely several times, but this only further embittered a nature that was inherently quarrelsome. One of Louis's hands was withering. He decided to go to Barèges, a spa in the Pyrenees, to take a cure, and wanted his young wife to accompany him. Hortense, who was showing signs of pregnancy, refused to go, and both her physician and her mother also opposed the journey.

When the Bonapartes learned of Hortense's pregnancy they circulated, in their alarm, outrageous stories, even going so far as to suggest that there had been intimate relations between the First Consul and his stepdaughter, a liaison, they maintained, favored by Josephine herself!

# 7

## Josephine's Fears

IN HIS WORK of consolidating power, the First Consul achieved many remarkable things during the years 1801 and 1802, but perhaps no achievement was greater than the peace he signed with the Roman Catholic Church. This Concordat disarmed his bitterest enemies—the royalists—both at home and abroad, and removed the last obstacle in Bonaparte's path to the throne.

The Constituent Assembly in 1792 had outlawed the Church, depriving it of power and properties. To most people's minds the Republic was synonymous with atheism; and by the same token monarchy, which in France meant the Bourbons, was synonymous with Roman Catholicism. The people were becoming weary not only of war but of a republican form of government. They longed for a monarch who would bring stability and peace after too many years of war, but they also wanted to keep some of the privileges the Republic had given them. By the terms of the Concordat of July, 1801, the Church's privileges were partially restored, but under many restrictions enforced by the Republic. The Church (and the royalists) were now under the standard of the new government, which, since the Brumaire *coup d'état*, was in Bonaparte's hands.

The negotiations with the Papacy were long and arduous,

for the restoration of the Church's privileges held many complications. But on Easter Day, 1802—a month after the Treaty of Amiens had been concluded with England—the Concordat was made publicly official.

The promulgation of the Concordat was celebrated with a solemn *Te Deum* mass at the Cathedral of Notre Dame. Significantly, the French cardinal who preached the sermon, comparing Bonaparte to Charlemagne, was Cardinal de Boisgelin who, twenty-five years before, had officiated at the coronation of Louis XVI.

On this great occasion the splendid new green livery of the First Consul's household staff attracted much favorable attention. But perhaps, in the midst of the pageantry, Josephine was even more striking, as she stood with Hortense and Bonaparte's sisters, surrounded by eighty young girls dressed in pastel colors. In the vast nave of the cathedral, they were like a basket of flowers.

This diplomatic achievement of Bonaparte crowned a year of brilliant show of executive power. Under the First Consul's close supervision, the French Institute had been reorganized, the Civil Code drawn up, and the entire system of higher education revised. Now, with royalist opposition eliminated and peace signed with England, France could look forward to years of prosperity.

It was the second consul, Cambacérès, who suggested having Napoleon Bonaparte elected by popular vote as consul for life, with the right to choose his successor. The plebiscite took place on August 2, 1802, and three and a half million people registered their approval. There were fewer than ten thousand dissenting votes.

The phrase, "the right to choose his successor," revived all Josephine's fears over not having produced a son and heir. It also stimulated her enemies to new plotting against her.

Bonaparte, as if oblivious to his heirlessness, was busily engaged in settling questions of protocol. General Duroc, as grand marshal of the Tuileries, was put in charge of palace expenditures and made director of the police. Four prefects were appointed to supervise the household, regulate etiquette, and superintend entertainments. Four ladies in waiting, called "ladies of the palace," were appointed to accompany Madame Bonaparte, and to present the wives of ambassadors to her. All these appointments were made from the nobility.

Bonaparte received ambassadors and foreign dignitaries in the large reception rooms that formed part of Josephine's apartments. But the throng was often uncomfortably dense.

That summer Bonaparte and Josephine settled in Malmaison, which had been greatly enlarged. Their household staff increased along with the number of guests to be entertained. The reception rooms on the ground floor were entirely redecorated and furnished under the direction of the artists François Gérard and Girodet-Trioson. The walls of the dining room were painted with allegorical figures. A study for Bonaparte was furnished in a room overlooking the garden. On the second floor a narrow tiled corridor separated the various suites of private rooms. The third floor accommodated the officers of the household.

Bonaparte considered the gardens and park too small, and bought up additional property. Mademoiselle Julien, who owned the estate of Bois-Préau, which "strangled" Malmaison, refused to sell, but other adjacent properties were acquired: the Jonchère, in which Eugène lived; the Butard, which was turned into a shooting lodge; the Clos-Toutain; the Chaussée; Saint-Cucufa; and the château and park of Buzenval. This made the entire estate extend from Rueil to Bougival, a stretch of land lying between the slopes of Suresne and Saint-Germain.

Always haunted by Marie Antoinette, Josephine had, at Malmaison, her own Trianon, where she reigned over a domain of exotic birds, animals, and flowers, the colors and perfumes of which must often have reminded her of her native land. Mallard ducks and black-and-white swans swam on the pond. Egyptian gazelles ran free in the garden, in view of Bonaparte's study. The shrieks of monkeys and the cooing of Moloccan pigeons mingled with the chattering of parakeets. Roses and tulips, brought at great expense from Holland, bloomed in the gardens and hothouses. The lily of the Nile, the rose of Damiette, the violet of Parma, rhododendrons, and camelias flourished with masses of hydrangea. The penetrating perfumes of the orange and lemon trees mingled with the sweeter perfume of the jasmine of Martinique.

At Malmaison, Bonaparte followed the work program he had adopted in Paris, rising at dawn and working through the day till dinnertime. His wife and guests followed a more leisurely routine.

Josephine breakfasted at eleven o'clock in her little circular drawing room, which opened out on the courtyard. There were sometimes women guests for this occasion, but never men, except Eugène or an occasional visiting relative like Joseph or Lucien. Eugène was now resplendent in a general's uniform, the commander of a cavalry battalion of the Guard. After breakfast, there was conversation or billiards, or reading the newspapers. Josephine passed her day changing costumes several times, receiving callers, adding marginal notes to petitions, or going for a horseback ride with Hortense.

Dinner was at six. The most frequent guests at this time were Murat, Duroc, Talleyrand, and Junot, among a dazzling array of ministers, artists, poets, scholars, and military men. The artist Isabey often dined with the Bonapartes, for he was at work on a portrait of Bonaparte. And the Marquis de Caulaincourt continued to put in regular appearances.

After dinner there were strolls in the park, with Josephine on Bonaparte's arm, and then, like good, solid citizens of Paris, an early retirement. Bonaparte went to bed first, soon followed by Josephine who often read aloud to him. She read aloud with the same charm that she did everything.

On Wednesdays, Madame Bonaparte gave large dinner parties for statesmen and generals. Cambacérès, the second consul of France, was usually there. The women, many of whom were young and pretty, were most often dressed in white, for this was the period when the styles of ancient Greece and Rome were in fashion. Every week or so, a small dance was given, and there were frequent theatricals in which Hortense and Caroline took leading parts.

Sometimes, in fine, warm weather, dinner was served in the park. But there was never any loitering at the table, for Bonaparte liked to play games when he was in a good humor. He particularly liked prisoner's base, and he cheated at this game as he did at cards. He can be pictured in shirt sleeves, pursued by Madame Junot or perhaps Hortense, tripping them up as they are about to catch him, or suddenly falling to the ground himself and then getting up with a roar of hearty laughter. Josephine did not engage in these romps but enjoyed watching her husband, laughing at his boyish pranks.

One evening as Josephine was strolling in the park with her niece Émilie de La Valette, she saw two badly dressed men approaching on the roadway. The sudden fear that they might be assassins who would make another attempt on Bonaparte's life flashed through her mind, and she asked Émilie to fetch La Valette or Eugène quickly. The two strange men drew near and stopped, gazing intently at Bonaparte who was playing games in the park with some companions.

"Do you want something, citizens?" Josephine asked in a trembling voice.

"Oh, heavens, no, citizeness. We are just looking. Are we trespassing?"

"Of course not! But..."

"Oh, you wonder why we stare at the General-Consul? Why, it's just, as I was saying to my brother, that it's amazing to see the ruler of the Republic enjoying himself like any poor, humble citizen."

They were interrupted by the arrival of Colonel Rapp, whom Émilie de La Valette had sent to help. After some rather ruthless questioning by Rapp, it was learned that one of the two men was a former artillery sergeant who had lost an arm at Marengo. At this point Eugène appeared and cleared up the confusion. He at once recognized one of the men as having served under him in Italy, and gently drew out the story of his life since an Austrian bullet had maimed him. The old pensioner had come to see the General-Consul, but he pointed to his younger companion and said, "Sir, I crave a horse and rifle for my brother. You'll see what he can do with them. . . ." He stopped, for Bonaparte had approached and greeted him so cordially that his eyes filled with tears.

Bonaparte immediately told Eugène to make provision for the two men. Then, putting his arm around Josephine's waist, he walked back toward the château.

As the two men sat with Eugène over a bottle of wine, the old sergeant proposed a toast to "the General-Consul." Then, setting down his empty glass, he said to his young brother: "Remember that the citizeness with the yellow hat is the mother of the Commandant here. I'll say no more to ye than that."

That evening Eugène went back to Paris, the First Consul withdrew to his study, and Josephine was left with Madame Junot, the La Valettes, and Colonel Rapp. The conversation dwelt exclusively on the various attempts on Bonaparte's life; for Josephine, despite all assurances to the contrary, was still pale and trembling from fright at the unexpected visit of the two men. She wept as she kissed Laure Junot good night.

"The face of that old soldier made such a terrible impression on me," she said, "that I am sure I'll not sleep tonight. If I say anything about it to Bonaparte, he'll be angry. He always tells me there's nothing to fear . . ."

Toward midnight, when everyone in the château was asleep, there was the sound of gunfire. Everyone was aroused in fear, women in nightgowns, half-dressed men. Bonaparte, in a dressing gown and holding a candle, tried to maintain calm by shouting in a loud voice, "It's nothing! Don't be afraid!"

He calmly issued orders for a search, and not long afterward Colonel Rapp returned from the park with another officer, bringing reassuring news. While crossing the lawn, a guardsman's horse had caught its hoof in a molehill and fallen. The shock of the fall had set off the guard's rifle.

Bonaparte, laughing heartily as he went to the landing of the main staircase, called out, "Josephine, cry no more! A mole is the cause of the excitement! Good night, ladies. Go back to bed and sleep well."

Josephine's state of tension at this time is described by the Duchesse d'Abrantès (Laure Junot) in her spiteful *Mémoires*.

Not long after buying the Butard property, Bonaparte wanted to show Josephine the charming hunting lodge that had originally been built for Madame de Pompadour. Josephine was suffering from migraine and didn't want to go, but Bonaparte insisted. "The fresh air will do you good," he said. "It's the best remedy for all ills."

Reluctantly, and still in pain, Josephine took her place in a barouche with Laure Junot. Bonaparte galloped ahead on horseback, chatting with Bourrienne (who had not yet fallen into disfavor), joking and apparently as happy as a schoolboy on a holiday. From time to time he rode back to the carriage to kiss Josephine's hand, or smile at her, and then he would ride on again, sometimes shrilling a silly, off-key song.

When they came to a brook with steep banks that promised a difficult crossing, Josephine refused to go farther. She said she felt as if she were on the edge of a precipice. "I cannot go to Butard by this road," she said to the groom. "Go tell the First Consul that I am returning to the château."

The horses had just been turned around when Bonaparte

came up, and over his wife's pleas and protests obliged the coachman to retake the road. He directed first from the near side of the brook, then jumped it with his horse and dismounted. "Come, come, with a good pull, and easing the reins, you'll make it," he said.

"No, no," Josephine shrieked in terror. "Let me get out, Bonaparte! Please, please! Have pity, let me get out!"

She was sobbing, her hands were clenched, and she was really a pitiful sight.

Bonaparte only shrugged. "Stop behaving like a child!" he said, in a displeased voice. "You shall cross the brook, and in the barouche!"

In order to put him in the wrong, Laure, who was pregnant, also asked permission to get out of the carriage.

"You're right," said Bonaparte. "A sudden jar might do you harm." And he himself helped her to set foot on the ground.

Emboldened by his kindness, Laure pleaded Josephine's cause, adding, "After all, if she were in my condition . . ."

Bonaparte would not let her finish, and his incredulous look made her give in to an irresistible giggling spell. He, too, was overcome with laughter, but he soon controlled himself and in a tone that tolerated only obedience, he ordered the coachman: "Pull up the steps. Let the barouche pass!"

He helped Laure cross the brook on some stones that made a path, while Josephine continued to weep and implore the coachman to wait.

"What now, fellow!" exclaimed Bonaparte, seeing the carriage still motionless. He brought his whip down furiously on the coachman's back. "Will you execute my orders?" he shouted.

The coachman hesitated no more, and whipped up the horses. The carriage crossed the "precipice," but not without a jolt and with some damage.

Josephine's face was so contracted with fear that it lost

all charm. Her eyes were reddened and puffy, and she looked positively ugly. As if aware of this, she drew her veil down over her face.

As soon as they reached Butard, Bonaparte assisted Josephine from the carriage rather roughly, and drew her off into the park to scold her. She took revenge by showering him with reproaches for his infidelities, naming singers and women of the palace, mentioning Laure and his assisting her across the brook.

"You're insane!" he replied harshly. "Your jealousy robs you of common sense." Then, softening, he bent his face down to hers, and said, as if addressing a child, "Come now. Kiss me and be quiet. You are ugly when you cry, as I've already told you."

# 8

## *The Pearl Necklace*

As SPRING WAS drawing to an end, Madame Bonaparte went again to Plombières, leaving Hortense, who was pregnant, to do the honors at Malmaison. In Hortense's circle of friends, all the young married women were pregnant. It was a safe society in which to leave Bonaparte. Very attached, now, to her husband, Josephine lived in constant fear that he would fall seriously in love with one of the women he met at Malmaison. When she heard that a charming actress, Mademoiselle Rolandeau, was there every Sunday, she could not refrain from mentioning it in a letter to Hortense that was full of complaints. To reassure her, Bonaparte wrote to his wife frequently.

On Prairial 30, Year XI [June 19, 1803], Bonaparte wrote: "We are sad here without you. . . . That big Eugène of yours arrived last night. He is in marvelous health. I love you as on the first day, because you are kinder and sweeter than anyone. . . . A thousand kind regards, and a loving kiss."

Twelve days later he wrote another affectionate letter: "Hortense is getting on well. Your big son was a little sick, but he is better now. I understand the ladies are going to perform *The Barber of Seville* tonight. The weather is very fine. I pray you to believe that nothing is truer than the affection I have for my little Josephine."

On the eighth of Messidor [June 27], he referred to her treatments at Plombières: "Your letter, dear little wife, informs me that you are not feeling well. Dr. Corvisart tells me this is a good sign, that the baths will have the desired effect and put you in fine condition. Nevertheless, it wrings my heart to know you are ill."

Finally, on the twelfth, he added:

"I see that you expect to return in a week. That will bring great pleasure to your friend who tires of being alone! Please believe that I love you, and am very impatient to see you again. Everything is sad here without you."

Upon her return to Malmaison, Josephine was able to attend a performance of *The Barber of Seville*. General Lauriston, the general and diplomat who had been selected to take the ratification of the Treaty of Amiens to England, played the part of Count Almaviva. Bourrienne, who had accompanied Bonaparte as his secretary to Egypt and back, played the role of Dr. Bartolo rather wittily, wearing a big wig and a black coat. General Savary, then a young man under thirty, took the part of l'Éveillé and, it is reported, "sneezed to perfection." Hortense played Rosina, sensitive and gay, her fair curls partly hidden by a pink-plumed black hat. Eugène was amusing as Basilio, and an officer by the name of Didelot was an acceptable Figaro. Laughter and applause greeted their efforts, and Josephine was proud of the success of Eugène and Hortense, the best actors of the improvised troupe.

Theatricals were the rage, and the Consul and his wife sometimes rode over to Lucien's château at Plessis-Chamant for performances of tragedies. Lucien had an emphatic, declamatory style. Much to Bonaparte's amusement, Caroline and Murat uttered their lines in strong Gascon accents. Elisa, who had been brought up at Saint-Cyr, spoke a pure French, but she had so many mannerisms, and went through such ridiculous contortions when reciting lines, that Bonaparte could not help laughing.

At Saint-Cloud, where Bonaparte installed himself in order to be nearer Paris in case of an emergency (dissension had again arisen between England and France, this time over Malta), there were sometimes professional performances, in which actors of renown took part: Talma the great tragedienne; the Olympian beauty, Mademoiselle George; and Mademoiselle Mars, who was then playing ingénue parts. Bonaparte was particularly impressed by the beauty and talents of Mademoiselle George.

During the autumn, the residence of the consular court alternated between the Tuileries and Saint-Cloud. Josephine agreed with Bonaparte that the Tuileries was a prison; it was impossible to draw a breath of fresh air at a window without drawing the attention of thousands of idle spectators.

In the palace of Saint-Cloud, as at Malmaison, Madame Bonaparte knew how to create a charming setting and atmosphere that showed off her own charms to best advantage. In the furnishings at Saint-Cloud she used a great deal of blue and gold, a flattering background for her lithe and graceful form, and for her misty gowns, always simple, and most often white with gold lamé borders. Josephine's arms and shoulders were always bare. Her hair was sometimes arranged in a golden snood; sometimes with bands of gold, as in the portrait by Prud'hon. When she first wore for Bonaparte the white and gold dress, her throat was encircled by a necklace in the form of a golden serpent. An enchanted Bonaparte kissed her shoulder. "Ah, Josephine," he said, "I'm jealous. You must have some plans! Why else are you so beautiful today?"

Her plans? To compete with her sisters-in-law. She easily succeeded in surpassing them in seductive beauty, despite their youth—Caroline and Pauline had just emerged from girlhood. She was also determined to charm Bonaparte, for he seemed to keep himself at a distance, confining himself to his rooms, which were separated from hers by the great corridor.

Whenever he wished to exercise his conjugal rights, Bonaparte undressed in his rooms, put on a lounging robe, wrapped his head in a turban of Madras cloth, and went down the long corridor to his wife, preceded by Constant, his valet, who carried a candelabrum. Usually he left her room toward eight o'clock in the morning. A few minutes afterward everyone in the château knew where Bonaparte had spent the night. Indeed, Josephine announced it to anyone who would listen, adding, with a happily fatigued air, clasping and unclasping her little hands, "So you see why I got up late today."

Madame Bonaparte remained in her rooms during the morning hours, receiving visitors, especially ladies of the old regime who had requests to make such as cancellations of debt or restitution of property. She welcomed them with great kindness, listened to their requests untiringly, and promised them everything they desired.

New faces were constantly to be seen in the blue drawing room of Saint-Cloud. Wives of generals or statesmen, recently married, came to pay their respects, enlarging Josephine's court. Madame Marmont, wife of the general, is described with particular admiration as a graceful and witty person. Several of these women were great beauties, particularly Mesdames Ney and Duchatel.

Toward six o'clock in the evening, the Consul usually went for a drive in an open carriage with his wife. More often than not there were guests for dinner. After Bonaparte went to bed, Josephine usually finished the evening playing billiards or backgammon.

It was to a little suite of rooms overlooking the Orangerie that Bonaparte had the actress, Mademoiselle George, brought to him. The young tragedienne pleased him as much by her lively wit as by her statuesque beauty. In Paris, the Consul received her in his own rooms on the mezzanine floor of the Tuileries, usually late in the evening. He no longer visited his wife's rooms except very late at night.

Josephine was informed of Mademoiselle George's visits by her footmen and, much upset and always alarmed, she would confide in Madame de Rémusat, whose advice she would listen to. She was sometimes so tormented with jealousy that she made odious accusations against the Bonaparte family and against her husband himself. Bonaparte, she told Madame de Rémusat, had no moral principles. He still masked his true character, but the time would come when he would abandon himself to all his vices. "Does he not feel that his position in the world permits him to satisfy all his desires?" she asked rhetorically. And she pondered another question: Would it not be to her enemies', the Bonapartes', advantage to bring about a gradual change in his private life and cut him off from all relations with her?

Exasperated by Josephine's complaints, the scenes she made and the tears she shed, the Consul several times said to her, "Imitate Livia, and you will find in me an Augustus." * "What does he mean by that?" she asked Joseph and Lucien. The two brothers merely smiled and repeated, "Imitate Livia."

In an effort to put an end to their quarrels, Bonaparte sent for Madame de Rémusat and talked to her about his marriage. "Josephine worries much more than she should," he said gravely. "She is always afraid I will fall seriously in love with another woman. Doesn't she know that I am not made for love? What does it matter to her if I indulge in certain distractions that in no way disturb my affections?"

The Consul's affection for "Georgina," however, threatened to endure. This was not a simple affair that would pass as

* The reference is to Livia Drusilla, who was first married to Tiberius and bore him two sons. Afterward she married Augustus and when their marriage produced no offspring she compelled him to divorce her (B.C. 38). She retained the affection of Augustus till his death. In short, Livia was a model Roman matron!

had the one with the singer Grassini, whose touching voice had charmed him; nor was it one of his "quarter-hour romances" that always ended as abruptly as they began. Josephine was in despair. If Georgina bore him a child, that would be the end. It would mean divorce; it would mean that her position in the world was lost. She had spies watch her husband, and she spied on him herself in an effort to catch the guilty pair.

The Consul, warned of this, took care not to be seen by Julie, Madame Bonaparte's maid, or by the other servants. When Josephine no longer knew what women were being entertained in her husband's secret room, she forgot all caution.

One night, as she kept Madame de Rémusat with her to unload all her griefs, her voice suddenly broke. She stood up and said, "I can't hold myself back any longer. Mademoiselle George must be up there now. I intend to catch them." When Madame de Rémusat tried to make her see that a lady of the palace could not go on such an errand, Josephine violently accused her of ingratitude and cowardice. Madame de Rémusat eventually accompanied her upstairs.

It was one o'clock in the morning, and everything was quiet in the palace. Silently, one behind the other, the two women climbed the secret stairway that led up to the Consul's rooms. Madame de Rémusat in the rear carried the candlestick. Suddenly there was a sound and Josephine, shuddering with fear, turned back. "Did you hear that?" she whispered. "It's someone who is standing guard. If it's Roustan, his Mameluke, he's capable of cutting our throats . . ."

Madame de Rémusat was so seized with fright that she ran down the stairs, still carrying the candlestick, leaving Madame Bonaparte in total darkness. Shortly afterward Josephine rejoined her in the drawing room and, upon seeing the frightened face of her deserter, burst out laughing. The laughter was infectious, and soon they were both overcome by it, ending the nocturnal expedition.

Some time later, the Consul invited Madame de Rémusat to dinner, seating her between himself and his wife. Toward the end of the meal, he asked a cryptic question: "What is your opinion on this: Should a husband submit to the demands of his wife and never share another bed but hers?"

Madame de Rémusat did not dare reply. She did not wish to displease the Consul, and she certainly did not want to displease Madame Bonaparte. At first she asserted that she had no opinion; she was only twenty, and really had not had enough experience to be able to judge. But the Consul would not let her off, so at last Madame de Rémusat cautiously said, "I could not say where the demands of a wife and the self-indulgence of a husband should stop. All the same, it seems to me it would be dangerous for the Consul to change his way of living, even slightly. It would cause some annoying gossip."

Bonaparte laughed and pinched her ear. "So," he said, "you are a woman. And you women all pull together."

It was a joyful day for Josephine that brought the news of the birth of Hortense's child. Little Napoleon Charles, as he was named, was for her a "guarantee against divorce." That delicate infant, she thought, would protect her from the intrigues, ambitions, and jealousies of the Bonaparte family, particularly if she could persuade Bonaparte to adopt him. The sole obstacle to this project, at least so she thought, was Louis's temperamental character, and he always opposed the wishes of his brother.

Louis demonstrated his touchy and suspicious character at once. Soon after the christening he announced that he was going to take his wife to Italy for the winter. Hortense categorically rejected the idea. She wanted to remain near her child, who was too young for such a long journey. So Louis departed alone, but as he said good-by he forbade her ever to spend a night at Saint-Cloud: "You may dine there, but if you sleep there, I warn you I'll get a separation."

Josephine was often to complain to her ladies in waiting about her son-in-law's mistrust that deprived her of one of her purest joys, having her daughter and grandson with her. It was because of his brothers' and sisters' outrageous insinuations, especially Lucien's, that Louis behaved in such a fashion toward Hortense, Josephine, and even Bonaparte. Yet, had not Bonaparte showered his family with benefits and honors? Had not Joseph and Lucien scandalously acquired wealth by taking advantage of their positions? Had not Bonaparte appointed them both senators? Still they opposed and thwarted him constantly!

Aided and abetted by Madame Letizia, Lucien had secretly married his mistress, that nonentity, the Jouberthon woman! Elisa and her husband, the mediocre Bacciochi, likewise took sides with the rebel. Pauline, who had accompanied her husband General Leclerc to Santo Domingo, was now back in Paris, a widow, and had already publicly compromised herself with Prince Borghese. Even Caroline and Murat, whose marriage Josephine had brought about against the Consul's wishes, did not spare their benefactress. As for Jérôme, the undisciplined playboy whom Bonaparte had sent to the West Indies, he had abandoned ship to go to the United States and marry a tradesman's daughter, Elizabeth Patterson, in Baltimore.

Even the Consul's Uncle Fesch was secretly against him, and Bonaparte had made him an archbishop and then a cardinal, after the former vicar had cast off his robes to amass a fortune "by looting Church properties in Corsica and by trading in Italian paintings!"

This was the way the Bonapartes repaid the Consul for his kindness and indulgences. It was only from his wife's family, from Hortense and Eugène, that Bonaparte received devotion and respect.

About this time there occurred an incident that opened Bonaparte's eyes to hidden talents of his very talented secretary, Bourrienne, and forced his replacement with a less brilliant but more honest secretary. Josephine was involved in Bourrienne's disgrace through her love for pearls.

Foncier, a well-known dealer in precious gems, often negotiated the purchase of rare jewels for Josephine. One day he offered her a necklace of pearls that was of incomparable beauty. Josephine was enthralled, but she hesitated because her debts, concealed partially from Bonaparte, were crushing. Yet how could she give up such a necklace? And how to ask Bonaparte for pearls? She knew he would reply as Louis XVI once had: "I would rather have a ship." She dared not incur one of his outbursts of wrath. Only recently General Duroc had been charged with finding out the total of her debts for Bonaparte, and she had refused to give him the facts. "Bonaparte will kill me if he finds out!" she had exclaimed. Then she had murmured some vague remark about paying them out of her "savings"!

The price Foncier set on his pearl necklace was 500,000 francs, an enormous sum at the time. Josephine went to Bourrienne for advice, and he promised to assume the responsibility of "arranging the affair." Bourrienne went about it so cleverly that Berthier, minister of war, handed over twice the sum to him, and the necklace passed into Josephine's hands.

Up to this point, everything had gone marvelously well. But now the problem was, how could she wear the pearls in front of Bonaparte, whose memory was so good and who had such a keen eye for her jewels and dress? Without confessing to Madame de Rémusat how she had paid for the pearls, Josephine confided her perplexity. "I don't know how I shall manage to wear them without Bonaparte's making a scene! And yet the necklace was a present from a man who was grateful to me for getting his son out of trouble."

Again she consulted Bourrienne, and one night her costume for the opera included the Foncier necklace.

"You look magnificent!" the Consul said, as he kissed her. "But what are these pearls? They seem to be extremely fine . . ."

"Why, yes, they are extremely fine," said Josephine, as Bourrienne had coached her. "You know them, you've seen them hundreds of times!"

"I've seen them?" Bonaparte exclaimed, staring at her in amazement.

"Of course you have," Josephine smiled, very self-assured. "They are the pearls that were presented to me by the Cisalpine Republic. Don't you remember? Ask Madame de Rémusat. Ask Bourrienne."

Madame de Rémusat merely nodded assent. Bourrienne was more loquacious in his confirmation of Madame Bonaparte's words.

"Astounding!" Bonaparte muttered, and said no more.

But not long thereafter Bourrienne was replaced, and Josephine pleaded in vain for the man who had rendered her so many services.

The Consulate had adopted as its emblem a sleeping lion. But now, the lion was awakening. On the seas, France had recovered the prestige she had enjoyed under her kings. And the British lion was roaring at the revival of the French fleet, and the vigorous rise of French commerce. On the other side of the Channel the realization grew that Bonaparte must be crushed if the war that had lasted more than twelve years, and which the Treaty of Amiens had not settled, were ever to end. For their purpose, the English appealed to the most intractable French elements—royalists still living in exile,

Bretons with their staunch support of the Bourbons, the most uncompromising Jacobins, the generals who were jealous of Bonaparte's rise to fame—and organized a gigantic manhunt.

Among the most useful malcontents were Georges Cadoudal, ardent royalist of the Vendée; General Charles Pichegru, who had escaped from French Guiana where he had been deported by the Directory; Armand and Jules de Polignac; and the Marquis de Rivière. They accepted the leadership of the ambitious General Moreau, victor at Hohenlinden, who had refused to acknowledge Bonaparte's supremacy and who wanted to succeed him in power. When Cadoudal became aware of Moreau's ambitions, however, he dissented; he was unwilling to struggle for the profit of another general. He wanted only to kill "the usurper" and restore the Bourbons to the throne of France.

Before giving the signal for the assassination, Cadoudal awaited the arrival of a prince of the royal house, the young Duc d'Enghien who was living in Baden near the Rhine. This hesitation caused the collapse of the conspiracy. It was the former minister of police, Fouché—deprived of his post for having opposed the election of the First Consul for life— who gave the alarm to Bonaparte, warning him "the air is full of daggers."

The leaders of the conspiracy were arrested one after the other: Moreau, Lajolais, Pichegru, Prince Armand de Polignac and his brother Jules, and finally the Marquis de Rivière and Georges Cadoudal. In March, 1804, the French police secretly crossed the Rhine, captured the Duc d'Enghien at Baden, and brought him first to Strasbourg and then to Vincennes.

Josephine's tears and pleas saved the lives of some of the chief conspirators, Moreau, the two Polignacs, and Rivière; but her pleas for the royal pretender were in vain.

On her way to Malmaison with Madame de Rémusat, Josephine told her of the arrest of the Duc d'Enghien and of her efforts in his behalf. Her face was very drawn and white.

"I have done what I could to make Bonaparte agree to let this prince live, but I'm afraid he has already made his decision."

"What! You think Bonaparte will have the duke executed?"

"I'm afraid so," said Josephine, shaking her head sadly.

The next morning she disclosed to Madame de Rémusat that she had once more pleaded for the young prince, but without success. The day passed mournfully.

That night after dinner, Bonaparte sat down to play with his little nephew, Napoleon Charles, and Madame de Rémusat concluded, as she watched him, that his gaiety was forced.

Suddenly Bonaparte looked at her fixedly. "Why have you not put on some rouge? You are quite pale."

"I forgot to," said Madame de Rémusat hesitantly.

"What?" The Consul laughed in disbelief. "A woman forgets to put on rouge?" Then, turning toward Madame Bonaparte, he added, "That would never happen to you, Josephine! Women find two things becoming to them— rouge and tears."

Both Josephine and Madame de Rémusat felt suddenly relieved. Surely the Consul was planning a scene of clemency. They were confident of it when they heard him murmur the lines from Corneille's tragedy, *Cinna*, with which Augustus forgives his would-be assassin: "Let us be friends, Cinna. 'Tis I who ask it."

But the next day, when Hortense arrived at Malmaison, she found her mother stricken by the news that the Duc d'Enghien had been shot.

"This is Bonaparte's first mistake," Josephine said, her eyes reddened by tears. "Until now, his glory was so pure! Who could have advised him to do it? He looked afflicted when he told me. That proves the execution was not by his orders. But when he saw my tears, he shouted at me: 'So you would like to see me assassinated!'"

Soon after this event, Josephine told her daughter that

Bonaparte intended to adopt Napoleon Charles. But that very evening Caroline told Hortense that the Bonapartes were aware of the Consul's plans to adopt the child and make him his heir.

"My brothers have more rights than your son," said Caroline, "and they will find a way to assert them."

"Oh, so many enemies already for a poor child still in his cradle!" Hortense murmured sadly.

Caroline's remark was confirmed when Louis, ill-advised by Joseph, wrote to the Consul that he would never consent to giving him his son.

The conspiracy against Bonaparte's life, and now the collapse of this plan, clearly revealed the precariousness of a government by life-consulship, and the need for establishing a dynasty with a clear line of succession. From the time the conspiracy was uncovered in February, the Consul and the Senate seriously studied the question, and two days before the execution of the Duc d'Enghien, the question was resolved. To preserve herself, France would return to government by hereditary monarchy.

Josephine's sterility was now a matter of State importance.

# Part III

## JOSEPHINE, EMPRESS OF THE FRENCH
### (1804-1809)

# 1

## *An Uncrowned Empress*

O<small>N THE</small> twenty-eighth of Floréal, Year XII [May 18, 1804], by unanimous vote of the Senate and a plebiscite, Bonaparte was proclaimed Napoleon, Emperor of the French. The Bonapartes urged him to divorce Josephine immediately. They objected to his idea of adopting Hortense's son, but they would welcome a new marriage. The hope that it would prove to be a childless marriage was not stated.

Napoleon displayed his irritation to Roederer, whom he was beginning to consult on many questions beyond economy and law: "What good apostles!" he exclaimed. "They tell me my wife is unfaithful, that her children's demonstrativeness is affected. My wife is a good woman who has never hurt them. At her age, poor thing, she needs only diamonds and pretty dresses to make her happy.... If I had been cast into prison instead of ascending a throne, she would have shared my misfortunes. It is right that she should share my grandeur.... She has always been persecuted by them.... I love Eugène and Hortense because they do everything to please me and sweeten my life. My existence would be unendurable without some sweetness in my domestic life!"

By the terms of the proclamation of the twenty-eighth of Floréal, Napoleon could adopt the children of his brothers when they reached the age of eighteen. In this way the Emperor retained the right to choose his successor.

It was at the château of Saint-Cloud that the Grand Chancellor Cambacérès, president of the Senate, came to salute the new Empress with the title of "Your Majesty." The guests at the dinner which followed had been instructed by Duroc, grand marshal of the palace, to address Joseph and Louis Bonaparte by the title of "Prince," and their wives by that of "Princess."

Elisa and Caroline (Mesdames Bacciochi and Murat), whose husbands were not brothers of the Emperor, did not have the right to the title of princess, and they were fiercely jealous. Every time the Emperor addressed Hortense as "Princess," Caroline's eyes filled with tears, and she had to drink several glasses of cold water in an effort to recover her calm.

The next day the two sisters went to the Emperor to complain, and the Emperor could not hide his amusement at their uncontrolled wrath.

"Listening to you," he exclaimed ironically, "one would think I had deprived you of your heritage from the late King, your father!"

Caroline was so upset that she fainted. The Emperor relented and dubbed his two sisters "Imperial Highnesses."

Madame Letizia was given the title of *"Madame Mère,"* mother of His Majesty the Emperor.

Josephine could not abandon the hope of bearing a son to Napoleon, and as soon as summer came, she once more set out for Plombières, this time accompanied by Madame de la Rochefoucauld. From Plombières she went to take the waters at Aix-la-Chapelle, where the Emperor joined her. She constantly complained of illnesses, constantly summoned Dr. Corvisart to demand remedy after remedy. The illustrious physician, to please her, prescribed all kinds of pills, some gilded, some silvered. They gave her great relief, she assured him; especially the pills he knew to have been made of bread crumbs.

After a voyage on the Rhine, and brief sojourns at Cologne, Bonn, and Mainz, where the streets were strewn with flowers for her, the Empress returned to Paris.

A few days after her return, Hortense gave birth to her second son, Napoleon Louis.

When Josephine learned that the Pope was leaving Rome to crown Napoleon in Paris, Josephine realized that her fate would soon be decided. Would she be crowned Empress? The Emperor did not mention it, and his silence disturbed her. He seemed to be undecided, and she knew that Joseph was urging him to divorce her.

Joseph argued eloquently. "Why crown Josephine, since you must sooner or later repudiate her?" he asked Napoleon. "The interests of France require that the Emperor have direct heirs. Would it not be better for the country, and for the Emperor himself, to place the dynasty of the Napoleons in the line of your own descent, rather than depend on the artificial succession established by the proclamation of the twenty-eighth of Floréal?" The coronation, he added meaningfully, would enable Napoleon "to marry whom he wished, to take as wife a foreign princess, or an heiress of a great titled family of France."

Napoleon turned these possibilities over in his mind, and occasionally words escaped him that made Josephine realize her imminent danger. Her fear made her lose all caution, and her ever-watchful jealousy almost brought about her ruin.

Above the suite of rooms he occupied at the palace of Saint-Cloud, Napoleon had a private apartment that communicated with his by a secret stairway. One day, when the Empress was as usual entertaining a great number of people in her drawing room, she noticed a woman whom she strongly suspected of having illicit relations with the Emperor slip away silently.

"I'm going to clear this thing up," Josephine said to Madame de Rémusat; and without heeding her friend's arguments she, too, left the drawing room. A half hour later she came back, very upset, and asked her companion to join her in her bedroom.

In a voice shaken with sobs, she said, "The Emperor was not in his study. I climbed the secret stairway, and the door of the small apartment above was shut. Through the keyhole I could hear the voices of Bonaparte and that woman.... I knocked, announcing myself. When they opened the door the disheveled condition they were in left no doubt.... I should have controlled myself, I know, but I couldn't, and I burst out with reproaches. The guilty woman began to cry, and Bonaparte got into such a violent rage that I just managed to escape him. He will come here, no doubt, and, I expect, make a terrible scene."

Madame de Rémusat had barely left her mistress when the Emperor stormed into the bedroom, furiously threatening her, breaking anything that came to hand. He had had enough of this spying! It must be stopped! And, without allowing himself to be mollified by Josephine's tears, he ordered her to leave Saint-Cloud.

The next day Napoleon summoned Eugène and informed him that he was going to divorce Josephine. He wanted a wife who could bear him children.

Eugène refused for himself and his mother the compensations offered by the Emperor. He said his mother would need consolation, and that he would go with her in her imposed banishment, even if it meant Martinique.

Hortense sought out Madame de Rémusat. "I dare not intervene," she said. "My husband has forbidden it. Anyway, if there is a chance of reconciliation, it will be in my mother's influence over Bonaparte with her sweetness and tears. We must let them work it out themselves . . ."

Hortense was right. Josephine's tears and meek submission disarmed the Emperor. But, after reassuring her, he again alarmed her by explaining the necessity for a divorce and trying again to persuade her to "imitate Livia."

"I cannot bring myself to take the initiative," he said. "If you show too much grief, if you yield to my will, I shall never find the strength to force you to leave me. And yet, I could wish that you might be able to do as the Roman empress did, in the interests of the State, and spare me of your own free will the difficulties of this painful situation."

Josephine did not have the greatness of soul it would have taken to give up a throne that the people of France apparently wished to deny her. She loved luxury too much, feared solitude too much, to bring herself to abandon society. The sacrifice was beyond her courage; she preferred to be complacent and submissive.

Moved by the thought of parting forever from a wife who was still dear to him, and overwhelmed with pity for Hortense and Eugène, the Emperor still hesitated, harassed by Joseph and Louis. But when he recognized the open joy of his brothers and sisters, he was shocked.

They were already boasting of having triumphed over his last scruples when Napoleon walked into Josephine's bedroom. He talked at length, sparing her no detail of the Bonapartes' attempts to bring about his separation from her. Then he took her, trembling, in his arms, kissing her and caressing her as if she were a child, and when he spoke again it was only to give a reassuring order:

"The Pope will soon arrive in Paris. He shall crown us *both*. Occupy yourself seriously with the preparations for the ceremony."

# 2

# A Heavy Crown

SOON AFTER HIS arrival at the château of Fontainebleau, where the Emperor and Empress were in residence, Pope Pius VII had a private conversation with the Empress, during which she confessed that her marriage had not been blessed by the Church. She asked the Holy Father to intercede with the Emperor and persuade him to have a religious ceremony performed. Josephine hoped in this way to allay forever her fear of divorce.

Napoleon had always evaded the issue, but faced with the firm will of the Supreme Pontiff, he realized he could no longer hold out and gave his consent. But he insisted that the religious rites must take place in the greatest secrecy, and that his uncle, Cardinal Fesch, must give the nuptial benediction.

In this way, the ceremony so long wished for by Josephine took place at Fontainebleau toward four o'clock in the afternoon of December 1, the day before the coronation in the Cathedral of Notre Dame.

December 2, 1804, is an amazing date in history. The events of that day amount almost to a deification, and cannot be adequately described.

That night the Emperor dined alone with the Empress,

and would not let her remove her crown. "No one," he said, "could wear the diadem with greater grace."

Exhausted but happy after the day of state ceremonies, Josephine compared in her mind the carriage of glass and gold that had carried her to Notre Dame with the fiacre that had borne her, four years before, from the Luxembourg to the Tuileries. In her mind's eye, she saw herself in her white satin robe with a train embroidered in silver and gold, resplendent with diamonds and pearls, passing between ranks of soldiers and an excited throng, to the brassy blare of military bands, the clanging of bells, the loud roar of cannons. She could see herself moving slowly toward the altar in her long, red velvet cloak embroidered with scattered golden bees, escorted by five princesses, the sisters and sisters-in-law of the Emperor. He stood there, waiting for her, his brow encircled with laurel. . . . Afterward there had been the *Veni Creator* while kneeling together before the Pope for the application of holy oil on the forehead and hands. Napoleon had taken the crown and, with his own hands, placed it on his head; then, with infinite tenderness, he set her crown upon his wife's head, as if to assure her that it would always be pleasant and easy to wear.

And that night it was pleasant and easy, for never had Napoleon been in a more delighted mood. All of Josephine's wishes were gratified. Married according to religious ritual, anointed by the Pope, crowned by the Emperor, she could believe at last that she had reached a haven of mercy, sheltered from all storms. But there was still one nagging worry . . .

Among the ladies of the palace there was one Josephine had treated with visible preference, praising her features, her taste and elegance. She was the blue-eyed, fair-haired Madame Duchatel, recently married to the director-general of the registry office who was thirty years her senior. No one danced, sang, or played the harp as well as she. . . . And how dazzling her little white teeth, how lingering the look in her dark-blue eyes! Moving with imperturbable calm and apparent indifference, she always attracted everyone's eyes, and at balls Prince Murat never left her side. She was a friend of Caroline; Eugène paid her court; and the Empress, because of her son, was particularly attentive to her.

During the ride to the Coronation, Madame Duchatel was the only woman who could not be accused of trying to engage the Emperor's interest. Her smile was only for Eugène, her pleasure was in his conversation.

That night, in his unusually relaxed mood, Napoleon lingered with the Empress and her ladies, after the Pope had retired to his rooms, chatting and jesting amiably with them. This was such a change in his habits that Josephine thought it must conceal some new intrigue. What woman was the cause of it?

She decided it must be Madame Ney, wife of the marshal of France and a former schoolmate of Hortense. Madame Ney was a pretty brunette, if rather thin; very proud of her rank but shy in the presence of the Emperor. Josephine began to watch her carefully and voiced her suspicions to Hortense. Hortense tried to appease her mother's fears and check her reproaches, which so wearied the Emperor.

But Josephine began weeping and accusing her husband, representing him as "the most promiscuous and immoral of men."

Napoleon, extremely irritated, declared to Hortense that her mother's jealousy made him ridiculous in the eyes of the world. "There is no stupidity that isn't attributed to me," he complained. "Do you imagine I don't know it? And it is her fault."

"No, Sire," Hortense said. "The fault lies with those who stir you up instead of soothing you. How can you expect more strength of my mother than you have? She suffers, she complains. It's natural. And if those who pretend to be your friends did not constantly run to you and repeat her complaints, or if you could manage to hide your discontent, happiness would return to you both, I am sure."

The Emperor, in a gentler tone, then alluded to Hortense's marriage and Louis's morbid jealousy. He began to laugh. "Louis," he said, "would have been quite happy married to the Empress. One would have stood guard at the door while the other stood guard at the window!"

Hortense talked to Madame Ney, who easily convinced her that she was not the Emperor's preoccupation. The guilty party, she asserted, was a lady of the palace whom Eugène courted, and whom Josephine for that reason treated especially well. Eugène was only "a screen." The lady was on the best of terms with Murat, or rather with Princesse Caroline, his wife, who was encouraging and directing the flirtation, fanning the Emperor's passion with the hope of injuring Josephine. The lady in question was Madame Duchatel.

Josephine soon found out that the Emperor visited Madame Duchatel in her bedroom at night. When all were asleep in the château, he crossed to her room barefooted, in breeches and shirt sleeves.

When warned that he was being spied upon, the Emperor rented a house on the Allée des Veuves for his new mistress, where he could visit her at his leisure.

Madame Duchatel maintained her reserved and innocent air, only paying more attention to her dress. The expression in her eyes seemed to have changed, to be more artful and sly, Josephine remarked to the Emperor; but he received the comment with bad grace, accusing her of objecting to trifling distractions.

Josephine, with difficulty, held back her tears, while Napoleon sat down at a card table and made up a game with Caroline, Madame de Rémusat, and Madame Duchatel. He chatted without glancing at his cards, holding forth pleasantly on the subjects of love and jealousy.

At the other end of the drawing room, the Empress sadly

went through the motions of playing whist, but her eyes never left the Emperor.

At a formal evening reception, held by the minister of war in celebration of the Coronation, Josephine was given new cause for uneasiness. As usual, only the ladies sat down to supper, while the gentlemen wandered at will among the tables. To anyone watching the Emperor as he passed among the ladies, bowing now to one, now to another, with a few words for each, it was obvious that "only one woman there attracted him, but he was taking care that it should not be noticeable."

The one woman, of course, was Madame Duchatel, beside whom he soon stopped to chat, leaning first on her chair and then on that of Laure Junot, who was sitting next to his favorite. Josephine saw him lean over the table and pass a dish of olives to Madame Duchatel.

Josephine questioned Madame Junot the next day on what Napoleon had said.

"Very little," Laure replied. "The Emperor advised Madame Duchatel not to eat olives in the evening."

Josephine did not pursue the subject, but remarked, "While he was at it, the Emperor should have told her it's ridiculous to act like Roxelane with a nose as long as hers." *

She then picked up a book from the mantelpiece, the latest romantic novel, *La Duchesse de La Vallière*, by the fashionable author, Madame de Genlis—a novel that was to be found at Saint-Cloud and Malmaison in every lady's room. Josephine opened it, saying, "This is a book that's turning the heads of all thin women with fair hair. They would all like to be favorites ..."

Her son's grief was added to her own. After having responded very favorably to Eugène's advances, Madame

---

* Roxelane, born a slave, became Sultaness of Suliman II.

Duchatel now avoided him or treated him with disdain, completely absorbed in her "dazzling conquest." And Napoleon, no doubt because of something she had told him, treated his stepson coldly. Eugène maintained a surface calm, but he was deeply hurt. Hortense, aware of this, also grieved in silence.

Josephine sometimes burst out in anger. During a violent scene with the Emperor, she declared she did not wish to receive Madame Duchatel any more. Napoleon left in a rage, and the next day accosted Madame de Rémusat rudely, accusing her of submitting too easily to the Empress's whims. Madame de Rémusat strongly denied it.

"If you do not approve of the inquisition the Empress is conducting against me," said Napoleon, "why can't you restrain her? She humiliates us both by this espionage. She furnishes arms to my enemies by acting this way. Since you are in her confidence, you must answer to me. I blame you for all her faults."

Madame de Rémusat protested that she was "incapable of leading the Empress astray." Then, growing bolder, she blamed Napoleon. He showed very little skill, she said, in his handling of the Empress; he was too brusk and rude with her.

This interview lasted so long that Napoleon seemed to have forgotten that he was giving a hunting party that day in the Bois de Boulogne. Josephine, who was waiting for him with her court, dispatched a groom to the Tuileries to find out what was keeping him. When told that the Emperor was closeted with Madame de Rémusat, she hurried in alarm to the Tuileries, but arrived after her friend had left.

She accused Madame de Rémusat at the first opportunity of "siding with the stronger," and of being a false friend. From then on, she treated Madame de Rémusat with noticeable coolness.

Eugène and Hortense were convinced that Madame de Rémusat had betrayed their mother, and showed marked disapproval. Madame Duchatel was anxious too, believing that an effort was being made to supplant her; and she soon managed to turn the Emperor against Josephine's companion, whom she regarded as a rival. Madame de Rémusat was definitely out of favor.

Meanwhile, however, the Empress calmed down. Napoleon, grateful for a respite, confessed his affair with Madame Duchatel, but insisted that it was only "a passing fancy. By tormenting us, you will prolong it. If you give me free rein, it will soon be over."

The Empress resigned herself to waiting and hoping. But she no longer spoke to Madame Duchatel. Far from being upset by the snub, the favorite felt she had triumphed—as did her counselor, Caroline Murat.

In the middle of winter, Eugène received orders to leave with his regiment for Italy. Josephine blamed the orders on the Bonapartes' jealousy and the machinations of the "official mistress."

Madame Duchatel was more emboldened by such success. Rather than appear embarrassed in the presence of the Empress, she "seemed to delight in her troubles." And Napoleon, during a short stay at Malmaison, threw off all restraint, and went openly for strolls in the park with Madame Duchatel and the young and discreet Madame Savary.

Josephine spent the days weeping, shut up in her bedroom, brooding over her imminent downfall, the divorce that was threatening anew. She was so overwhelmed that she said nothing, feeling that her complaints would be useless. Her resigned melancholy, her mute suffering, finally touched the Emperor.

"Be reassured," he said gently one day when he found her alone, her eyes filled with tears. "I was smitten, but I am no longer."

For one thing, he had seen through Caroline's plot; and he confided to Josephine his realization that "they" were trying to rule him by slandering those closest to him. He went into the most intimate details, and declared that he wanted to break up an affair that no longer gave him pleasure. He even asked Josephine to help him! His wife was not vindictive, Napoleon well knew.

"With me, she has always been defenseless," he said to Lucien one day.

Assured that the danger was over, Josephine's fears melted, and all idea of vengeance disappeared. She was ready to forgive a woman who had hurt her deeply, and when she summoned Madame Duchatel she talked to her kindly. She merely reproached her for her imprudence, which she laid at the doors of youth and inexperience; and advised her to act with more reserve in the future. She promised to forget the incident and reinstate her in favor.

Far from being grateful for such moderation, Madame Duchatel declared loftily that her conduct in no way deserved such reproaches, and for several days she preserved a cold and haughty mien.

From then on, the Emperor avoided speaking with his former favorite, or even looking at her. He took Josephine back into his confidence, made Eugène a general, Prince of the Empire and Grand Chancellor of State, with the title of Serene Highness.

The Bonapartes' intrigues again had borne no fruit.

# 3

## Wife of a Kingmaker

Never had Josephine been more compliant to her husband's wishes, more sympathetic or devoted. She now accompanied him everywhere. Nothing could keep her from his side, neither privation nor fatigue. If he refused to take her with him, she used clever strategy. When he departed in the middle of the night, he would find her sitting in his carriage, laughing at his surprise.

"But it's impossible. You cannot come," he scolded her. "I'm going too far. You'd have to put up with too many difficulties."

"I'm not the least bit afraid," she replied, smiling.

"But I must leave immediately."

"I'm all ready."

"But you will need a great deal of luggage—"

"No more than is here."

More often than not, the Emperor gave in, as in April, 1805, when he went to Milan to accept the Italian crown.

Josephine took with her a small court, consisting of the four ladies of the palace, Mesdames de la Rochefoucauld, d'Arberg, de Serrant, and Savary; several chamberlains and officers of rank; her little chest of jewels; and her dog.

The ceremony took place in the Cathedral of Milan on May 26, and Josephine and her court watched from the gallery. A thrill of pride went through her as she saw Napoleon set the iron crown of the Lombard kings on his head, and heard him repeat in a loud voice the ancient formula: "Heaven bestows it, woe be he who touches it!" *

She was even prouder in June, when the Emperor entrusted the administration of his new realm to Prince Eugène, as Viceroy. Her pride was not unmixed with sadness, for it meant separation from her son.

That same month, still pursuing a policy of reckless violation of the Treaty of Lunéville, Napoleon awarded the republics of Lucca and Piombino, as one principality, to Elisa Bonaparte and her husband Felice Bacciochi.

In the midst of the entertainments and state functions at Milan, Josephine noticed that the Emperor was enjoying a flirtation with one of her ladies in waiting, Mademoiselle Lacoste. After a violent quarrel, the Empress obtained the dismissal of the young woman in question ...

The creation of the Kingdom of Italy and the annexation of Genoa to the French Empire filled England with anxiety. The Third Coalition of world powers was formed to oppose the Emperor, and without preliminary negotiations or a declaration of war, Austria invaded Bavaria and advanced toward the Rhine.

Napoleon immediately sent his chamberlain, Monsieur de Rémusat, to Strasbourg, to prepare a residence for the Imperial couple. Wishing to be with her husband, and to escape the unfriendly society of the Bonaparte family and the boredom of Saint-Cloud, Josephine had persuaded the Emperor to let her follow him at least as far as Strasbourg, while he took command of the Grand Army and fought his battles on the Rhine.

Toward the middle of October, she received a letter from

---

* The words in Italian are: *Il cielo me la diede, guai a chi la toccherà!*

Napoleon announcing his entry into Munich: "The enemy is beaten, routed, bewildered. Everything gives promise of a fortunate campaign, one of the shortest and most brilliant . . ."

He was right. Within a month Josephine heard, successively, of the capitulation of Memmingen, the victories of Elchingen and Ulm, and the entrance of the Grand Army into Vienna.

At his orders, she went to Baden, Stuttgart, and then Munich, where she received the news of the great victory of Austerlitz.

A few days after Christmas, Napoleon rejoined Josephine, and the weeks that followed were busy. Bavarian troops had fought side by side with the French at the battles of Ulm and Austerlitz, and as their reward, Napoleon declared the Electorate of Bavaria a principality and made the Elector King. At the same time he legally adopted Prince Eugène, the Viceroy of Italy, as his son, and negotiated a marriage between him and Princess Augusta, daughter of Maximilian I, the new-made King of Bavaria.

The various ceremonies, however, did not pass without some heartaches. The Princess Augusta had previously been affianced to Charles, the hereditary prince of Baden. To get rid of him, Napoleon promised him a substitute bride: Josephine's niece, Stéphanie de Beauharnais.

When Eugène arrived in Munich three days before his marriage, which took place on January 14, 1806, he went first to the Emperor without pausing to call upon his mother. Josephine, hurt and annoyed at his apparent lack of eagerness to see her, was giving way to her grief when the Emperor appeared, pushing Eugène ahead of him into the room: "Look, Madame," he said, "here is your great ninny of a son!"

The newlyweds took the road to Italy, and the Emperor and Empress returned to Paris.

When Josephine saw Hortense, she felt a pang. Her daughter's face was drawn and thin. Hortense had lost weight, and was obviously worried about something. Questions drew out the story: Louis had forbidden her to attend Eugène's wedding. Hortense maintained that this was the only reason for her sadness. She was afraid to alarm her mother by telling her the whole truth about Louis's maltreatment. And she was careful not to reveal to Josephine what she still scarcely dared confess to herself: that for a long time she had been in love, while struggling against it, with a young captain of Dragoons, the handsome Comte Charles de Flahaut.

One night Napoleon, whose eyes missed nothing, spoke to Josephine about Hortense. "She looks far from well," he said. "Louis does not make her happy. We may have bad moments ahead. If she were to fall in love, it would be violently. And love produces great follies."

Josephine declared she was not worried about that; Hortense was reasonable and self-controlled.

"Don't be too sure," said Napoleon. "Everything about her reveals a passionate nature. Watch her attitudes, her words. She is in every way your daughter."

Josephine was relieved when Hortense's sadness disappeared. Now all was well, and she could enjoy her happiness. Content with her son's destiny, she lived in a state of freedom from care, of happy indifference. She felt calm, appeased, as if nothing could ever hurt her again. Never had she been surrounded with so much kindness and affability. She sought no pleasures. dreaded no pains.

No thought or action of the Emperor escaped her. She "followed, noticed, guessed everything," but remained gentle, gracious, and serene, avoiding all disputes with him. Convinced that he had neither the time nor the temperament for a great love affair, she accepted his infidelities without revolt.

Her constant efforts to please him, however, made her life "an uninterrupted battle of coquetry." To convince him that no one understood him as she did, she studied his attitudes and expressions. To secure his admiration, she spent long hours selecting her clothes, and would inspect her face in the mirror for hours at a time. With creams, powder, and rouge, she did everything possible to banish the signs of age from her face, and give it an illusion of youthful freshness. Ill-natured gossip said that she carried her indulgence of her husband's infidelities so far as to promote his passing fancies. Young women, selected from the middle-class citizenry, were always posted in the drawing room outside the Emperor's suite. When the Empress passed, they opened the doors and announced her, just as they did for the Emperor. The prettiest of these *dames d'annonce* often attracted the eyes of the Emperor, but the Empress was in no way offended.

Josephine heard that Napoleon was even seeing Madame Duchatel again, but she stifled her jealousy. Convinced that Napoleon could have no offspring, she shut her eyes to this affair as to the discreet court he was paying to another young protégée of Princesse Caroline, Éléonore de la Plaigne.

Éléonore had been educated at Madame Campan's, and had been married for a year to a certain Revel, supposedly an army officer but actually a complete rogue. This singular husband had vanished the day after the wedding, and two months later was arrested for passing counterfeit bills of exchange, and imprisoned. Caroline found a home for the deserted young bride, first at Chantilly, then at a small house in Neuilly, where she was awaiting the annulment of her marriage. Tall, graceful, beautiful, and far from shy, Éléonore de la Plaigne happened to be at Murat's one day when the Emperor came to lunch. Certain propositions were made to her, which she in no way repulsed, and for some time the Emperor had been visiting her at her house in Neuilly. Now he was receiving her secretly at the Tuileries. Josephine shut her eyes . . .

On March 2, 1806, Napoleon adopted Stéphanie de Beauharnais, granddaughter of the poetess Fanny and his wife's niece, and set the date, April 7, for her marriage to Prince

Charles of Baden. Stéphanie, who had also been educated at Madame Campan's, had been a frequent visitor to the Tuileries; now, while waiting for her marriage, she had her own suite of rooms there. Pretty, fair-haired, gay and witty, she was much admired at court, and especially by the Emperor.

The Bonapartes worried a great deal over the favors he granted her. What was he thinking of, they demanded, to allow such a young girl to pass *immediately after* the Empress? Caroline was particularly envious and addressed some harsh words to Stéphanie, trying to humiliate her. The unimpressed girl only laughed at Caroline's haughty air, and made the Emperor laugh with her.

Prince Charles of Baden was ugly, stupid, and disagreeable. For the wedding, he had his hair cut Roman fashion, which made him look more ridiculous than ever, and Stéphanie forbade him to come near her. The wedding night was an unhappy one for the groom; despite his supplications he was obliged to spend the night in an armchair without having touched his bride.

Napoleon was highly amused when he heard of this, and he seemed to take pleasure in the flirtations of his adopted daughter. Josephine was finally annoyed and preached to her niece. A subdued Stéphanie agreed to go to Baden with her husband, but shed many tears over leaving France.

To satisfy the ambitions of his family and to consolidate his rule, Napoleon bestowed many titles upon them that year. Murat was made Duc de Clèves et de Berg. Joseph was made King of Naples and Sicily. Pauline and her new husband, Prince Borghese, were made Duc and Duchesse de Guastalla.

The Bacciochis had reigned for some time as Prince and Princesse de Piombino, and Elisa was displaying some ability to rule. Lucien, disgraced and exiled for flatly refusing to repudiate the wife of his choice, Madame Jouberthon, was living in Rome. Jérôme's American wife had borne him a son in England, but Napoleon still refused to recognize the marriage, even though he had made his brother a Prince of France, and given him command of a division of South Germans in the recent campaign. It was clear that when the delinquent Jérôme came to heel and repudiated his Baltimore wife, he, too, would have his reward.

As Caroline was leaving for her Duchy of Clèves, she learned that the Emperor had proclaimed Louis, King of Holland. She ran to Hortense at once.

"I certainly hope you'll not accept?" she said curtly. "The Emperor promised *me* that crown!"

Hortense had no desire to leave France. She dreaded the idea of being so far from her mother and the Emperor, at the mercy of Louis's morbid jealousy in a foreign land. But Napoleon refused to reconsider, and to avoid testing his compassion, he cut short the farewells between Hortense and her mother.

After the departure of her daughter and grandsons, Josephine went into a kind of collapse for several days. The Bonapartes, now at a distance from Paris, could no longer torment her; but she would still miss the comfort of her children.

"My dear Eugène," she wrote to her son in August, "it took me some time to recover from my stricken feelings over your sister's departure. I felt again the grief I experienced when you went away, and I was too upset and ill to write . . ."

# 4

## *The Day of an Empress*

MALMAISON was definitely too small for an Imperial court, and Josephine had to resign herself to follow the Emperor to Saint-Cloud, Fontainebleau, and Rambouillet. Each of these residences had the same grave and noble settings, the same environment and people, the same settled habits.

The daily life in these palaces passed much as it did in the Tuileries, ceremoniously and uniformly, in formal reception rooms as in private suites, according to Napoleon's dictated wish. On days, however, when there was neither a meeting, a concert, nor a supper, the etiquette of the court was less rigorous than in Paris, and life was less monotonous.

In the Tuileries the rooms of state, called the Apartment of Honor, overlooked the Carrousel, at the corner of the Pavillon de Flore. In the antechamber, the porter, footmen, and court ushers were decorative in their green liveries. The first reception room was reserved for people of moderate importance, and beyond the orderlies' room and the pages' room was the Grand Salon, the great drawing room of the Empress that led to her private apartment.

Her private suite of rooms consisted of a small drawing room, a study, a library, a bedroom and boudoir, a bathroom and dressing room. A dark corridor separated the rooms over-

looking the garden from those overlooking the interior courtyard.

Narrow stairways led from the main floor to the mezzanine
and second floor, where the Emperor had his own suite of
rooms. At the entrance to this private suite the *dames
d'annonce* stood on duty; one of them guarded the door of
the Yellow Drawing Room and opened it only to ladies of
honor, or ladies who had been presented at court.

At Saint-Cloud, the state apartments were on the second
floor and communicated with the "grand apartment" of the
Emperor. The decoration there was less austere than that of
the Tuileries, and the suite of private rooms was pleasanter.
In the middle of the bedroom stood the gondola-shaped bed,
and mirrors brightened walls that were covered with "land-of-
Egypt-brown" velvet. A painted frieze in Greco-Roman style
ornamented the bathroom.

When the Emperor spent the night with the Empress in
her rooms, he arose between seven and eight o'clock, and
drank a cup of tea or an infusion of orange flowers before
leaving her. Josephine always tried to make him linger, but
he tore himself away from her arms after wrapping her in
the bedclothes, patting her on the face and shoulders, and
scattering kisses over her face and throat. He went off laughing,
calling her his "sweet fool."

Shortly afterward Josephine drank an herb tea or a lemon-
ade. Her favorite dog, a black Pomeranian from Vienna, was
then brought to her by Mademoiselle La Brisée, who was in
charge of it. After caressing and playing with her pet for a
while, Josephine got out of bed, toward nine o'clock, and went
into her dressing room.

Her lady of the bedchamber was Madame Mallet; and she
had four mistresses of the wardrobe: Mesdames Fourneau
and Charles, Mesdemoiselles Aubert and Avrillon, assisted
by the mulatto, Malvina. They were entrusted with the
Empress's lingerie, gowns, and jewels, and were treated by her

as friends. She told them her secrets, confessed to them her fears and hopes, and showed them her most precious letters. She never reproved them, and always treated them with great politeness, as she did all her ladies in waiting. If one of them were at fault in some way, the Empress addressed no word to her for a day or two, or several days, depending upon the misdemeanor.

After a long bath, Josephine would cream and powder her face. If she had shed tears or slept badly the night before, the powder would not stick and she would say: "You see, because I'm not feeling well I look as if I'd fallen in some flour!" She used no perfume because Napoleon would tolerate only *eau de Cologne* or lavender water. Twice a month the Empress called in her pedicurist, a German-Jew named Tobias Koen.

When she had completed her toilette, she donned a loose gown of muslin, Holland linen, batiste, or percale. Then her stockings were put on—very fine, white silk stockings, and close-fitting heelless slippers of soft colored leather or silk.

After being corsetted in dimity or percale, she changed into a long, lace-trimmed dressing gown, and her hair was combed and arranged. For important occasions the celebrated hairdresser, Duplan, was summoned, but ordinarily the footman Herbault performed the duty. Josephine's hair was still thick and abundant and, thanks to tinting, was a bright-chestnut hue. Most often her hair was arranged with a long curl hanging down on one shoulder, small curls over the forehead that gave her a childlike look, and a knot high in back that was held in place by bandeaux, recalling the coiffures of Greek sculpture.

While the Empress's hair was being arranged, the ladies of the palace and the wardrobe mistress came in carrying baskets of dresses, hats, and shawls. In summer the dresses were of white lawn or percale, exquisitely embroidered; in winter, of woolen cloth or velvet. Harmonizing with the dresses, the coats were trimmed with ermine or astrakhan, and lined with satin.

When Josephine had chosen her morning costume, which was always modestly high-necked, she put on a hat and, thus attired, entered the drawing room where her tradesmen were waiting: milliners, jewelers, dressmakers, cabinetmakers, manufacturers of stringed instruments, painters, sculptors, dealers in rare prints, and makers of mechanical toys, which she would give to her grandsons and nieces, or the children of the high officers of the Empire.

After the tradesmen had gone, the Empress received those who had been granted the favor of an audience. Then she wrote letters—to her son, her daughter, her friends.

Since her marriage to Alexandre de Beauharnais, Josephine had improved her spelling and handwriting. In order to play a worthy part during the Consulate, she had not stopped her studies. Now, more than ever, she must not make mistakes before visiting dignitaries. Abbé Halna taught her history and geography and Josephine applied herself studiously and absorbed all the necessary facts. A year of such study had been enough to acquaint her with everything that was happening in Europe. Surprised and flattered foreigners declared that she had "more knowledge than the princesses of the *ancien régime.*"

Before leaving her rooms, the Empress received her physician, Dr. Leclerc, who was succeeded at his death by Dr. Horeau. Always punctual, Josephine left her rooms at eleven o'clock, accompanied by one of the ladies of the palace, and entered the great Yellow Drawing Room where guests were presented to her: wives of high officers, generals, ministers, councilors of state. There were "never any foreigners and, naturally, never any men," she noted in a letter.

Luncheon followed, and little hunchbacked Madame de la Rochefoucauld, first lady in waiting, always added a cushion to Josephine's chair, which was already cushioned in violet satin. The menu included soup, hors-d'oeuvres, an entrée, roasts, a dessert course, and fruit, accompanied by Burgundy. Josephine scarcely touched her food, but devoted herself to her guests, tactfully putting them at their ease, and encouraged them to talk. In this way she learned the gossip that always delighted the Emperor.

After luncheon, the Empress retired to her drawing room, for needlework or a game of billiards with her ladies in waiting. She interrupted these occupations to greet persons admitted for an audience, members of the former royalist society or of the new society. Wishing to please everyone, she awarded positions, titles, pensions, and gratuities, addressed letters of recommendation to ministers, telling them about her protégés. Always calm and kind, she endured with a smile even the most importunate ones, and sent them away satisfied.

At five o'clock she had tea and distributed candies to children who were brought to see her, and who always went away bearing gifts. She then returned to her rooms to change her clothes, have her hair rearranged, and choose her gown for the evening. The Emperor sometimes came to watch her dress, teasing her attendants, pinching their cheeks and ears as he did the Empress, before leaving.

Dressing for evening took some time, for Josephine was always turned out with great elegance. Sometimes she wore flowers in her hair, sometimes pearls and precious stones, and her dress was always cut very low. Over her shoulders floated a little shawl, as light and filmy as possible.

At six o'clock, she saw the Emperor again for dinner. The table was sometimes set in his rooms, sometimes in hers. Footmen passed the food, and in fifteen or twenty minutes the meal was over. In Paris, except on Sundays when princes and princesses came to the family dinner table, Napoleon and Josephine dined tête à tête. At Saint-Cloud, at the Élysée (which had become a "country residence"), they sometimes invited a few officers of the Empire and their wives. Often, after dinner, the Emperor worked until nine or ten at night, but before he retired to work they had coffee, poured by the Empress, in the Yellow Drawing Room.

Josephine, who liked to sit up late at night, waited for him patiently, playing backgammon or whist with one of her chamberlains or a high dignitary.

Before going to bed, she again bathed and spent some time preparing her toilette for the night. According to Napoleon, she was as elegant and charming to look at in bed as at any other time.

Sometimes Napoleon wanted her to read aloud to him, and he fell asleep, "lulled by that musical voice of hers," which never ceased to delight him.

In the Emperor's absence, Josephine's life in Paris changed in no way. Napoleon was kept closely informed, and knew at once of any slight relaxation of the rules of etiquette. No matter how far away he might be, he would send a reprimand, always ending with, "Live as you do when I am in Paris," or, "If you alter the usual way of life, I shall be displeased." She obeyed with docility, always fearful of divorce.

For her personal expenditures, her pensions and charities, the Empress received an annual allowance of 480,000 francs. She gave assistance to many poor people, many colonials, even paying for the upbringing of their children. She bought works of art and objects of all kinds, which she gave away to those who seemed to covet them. Her clothes allowance, set at 360,000 francs, was always substantially overspent, and the Emperor was obliged to pay off the balance. Jewelers figured largely in her accounting too, for Josephine now possessed the most beautiful gems in the world: necklaces of pearls, turquoises, and rubies; a great set of diamonds, including coronet, crown, necklace, comb, earrings, bracelets, belts of rose diamonds, and a massive necklace that included eight strands of stones. Marie Antoinette's jewel chest, which had never been completely full, was not large enough to contain Josephine's jewels, and she constantly acquired new sets of jewels, loving just to accumulate them, to handle and contemplate them, and to show them to any who expressed an interest. "An endless shimmering stream" flowed through her fingers.

There were many who were quick to take advantage of her, and the Emperor laid down rules in an effort to check her extravagance and generosity. He forbade "any member of the household of Her Majesty the Empress to receive, in her rooms, furniture, paintings, jewels, and other effects delivered there by tradesmen or other individuals." But try as he would to reduce exaggerated prices, to lower the total of the bills presented, and to pay off the remaining balance, nothing could stop the mounting tide of Josephine's purchases and debts. He forbade the celebrated milliner, Mademoiselle Despeaux, entrance to Saint-Cloud. When she managed to slip into the Blue Drawing Room, he had her arrested, but let her go free at the end of the avenue. He thought he had frightened her off forever, but she came back, as did all the other tradesmen and beggers-for-favors who had been driven off in similar fashion. They returned, bolder and in larger numbers than ever.

# 5

## Josephine's Games of Patience

ENGLAND considered the Confederation of the Rhine intolerable, and in the summer of 1806 Napoleon's indomitable enemy formed a new coalition against him. Prussia, taking the initiative, called upon Napoleon to withdraw his troops from beyond the Rhine. As his only reply, the Emperor invaded Germany with the Grand Army.

Josephine accompanied him as far as Mainz, and before parting from her, he held her in his arms for a long time. "How painful it is," he said, "to leave the one you love best!" And as Josephine burst into tears and sobs, he was so overcome with grief in his turn that his departure had to be delayed. But he soon overcame his weakness, embraced his wife once more, and made her promise to wait for him in Mainz.

Queen Hortense came to stay with her mother for a while, and Stéphanie, the Princess of Baden, also paid a visit. But neither her daughter nor her niece could comfort Josephine in her sadness, nor dispel her anxieties. To add to her troubles, some of the ladies of her court, led by Madame de la Rochefoucauld, formed a "disdainful opposition," a clique which, upon hearing of the death of Prince Louis of Prussia at Saalfeld, flaunted a grief that shocked the Empress.

Josephine wrote often to Napoleon, always begging to let

her join him and follow him everywhere. She had no authority over a hostile court that, within her hearing, praised the Prussian army and doubted the successes of the French, and she wanted to leave Mainz.

After the battles of Jena and Lübeck in October-November, she implored the Emperor to let her leave. Her ladies in waiting found her constantly in tears. Napoleon was on the point of yielding to her demands and having her join him in Berlin, when the need to cross into Poland to surround the Russians forced him to give up the idea. From then on Josephine's sorrows increased, and her jealous fears were always with her.

"Polish women are so pretty!" she wrote the emperor. He reassured her: "All the Polish women here are Frenchwomen. Anyway, there is only one woman for me. Do you know who she is? I could give you a good portrait of her, but I would have to make it too flattering for you to recognize it . . ."

A few days later, on December 5, he joked about her continuing jealousy: "You tell me . . . that you are not jealous. I noticed long ago that choleric people always maintain they are not choleric; that those who are afraid often say they are not. You are therefore convicted of jealousy."

On the fifteenth, he added, "My dearest, I am leaving for Warsaw. In a fortnight I shall be back. I hope then to be able to call you to my side. All the same, if that's too long to wait, I should not at all object to your returning to Paris, where you are wanted. You well know that I depend on events . . ."

Two weeks later he was justifying himself again: "I laughed heartily over your last letters. You have an idea of Polish women's beauty that they don't deserve. . . . I read your letter in a drafty barn, full of mud and wind, and with straw for a bed. Tomorrow I shall be in Warsaw."

When he wrote this letter Napoleon was at Pultusk, and he had just received news that his mistress, Éléonore de la Plaigne, had given birth to his son, who had been christened Léon.

It was the next day, on the road to Warsaw, that he first met the Countess Marie Walewska. His carriage was passing through a small village when a beautiful and well-dressed young woman sprang forward, forcing the horses to stop. With tears in her lovely eyes, she took the Emperor's hand, kissed it, and implored him to save her country ...

They met again in Warsaw. Everything about Marie Walewska charmed him—her grace and sweetness, her natural timidity. He admired her, desired her, and loved her as he had not yet loved any woman ...

"The winter is cold," Napoleon wrote, in one of the many letters to his wife that were intended to check her impulse to join him in Warsaw. "The roads are bad and not very safe. I cannot agree therefore to let you expose yourself to such dangers and discomforts. Return to Paris for the winter; go to the Tuileries; give receptions; lead the same life you do when I am there. This is what I want you to do. I shall join you soon there, perhaps. But you must definitely not travel three hundred leagues in this season, across enemy territory, and behind the army."

Josephine persisted in her demands, and remained at Mainz, waiting for a summons that never came. Napoleon replied affectionately to her letters, but firmly maintained that the roads were impracticable, that the journey was too long and dangerous for her, and that she should return to Paris as soon as possible.

Finally, Josephine realized it was hopeless and returned to Paris to take up her usual life at the Tuileries.

Her sadness increased because her presentiments had been right. From Polish women recently arrived in Paris, Josephine heard about Marie Walewska and Napoleon's love for her.

She had one ray of hope. It was said that Napoleon, who had billeted his army at Liebstadt, was thinking of re-establishing the monarchy in Poland and giving the crown to Prince Eugène ...

To learn the future, she told her fortune with cards, and often played patience. Every night two packs of cards were placed in front of her, and she would play game after game. One day she worked out, in the presence of her ladies, the "great patience" and the "little patience," the "windmill," the "patience of fifteen," and several other variations. She wanted to find out whether a messenger would arrive before night.

The hours wore on and it was late, but Josephine kept the ladies, saying, "I cannot bring myself to go to bed without knowing whether some news will come." And she began another game of "great patience." Barely had she put down the last card on the last stack when Cambacérès, the Grand Chancellor of the Empire, entered and gave her a letter from Napoleon.

The letter had been written from the château of Fincken-stein where, Josephine knew, Madame Walewska was staying, but Napoleon only made fun of all his wife's fears, treating them as fantasies: "I don't understand what you say about ladies I associate with," he declared. "I love only my little Josephine, who is good, sulky, and capricious, who knows how to quarrel with grace, as she does everything; for she is always delightful, except when she is jealous . . ."

Sad news made Josephine momentarily forget her anxieties about her husband. A letter came from Holland telling her of the death of her grandson, Napoleon Charles. Overwhelmed with sorrow, but realizing that her daughter's sorrow must be even greater, she recovered her self-possession and at once set out for The Hague. Her strength failed her, however, near Brussels, and she interrupted her journey to rest a while at the château of Laeken. Hortense arrived there shortly after-ward, with her husband and second son, Napoleon Louis. The Empress, her face bathed in tears, sprang toward the Queen and embraced her impetuously. Hortense, dry-eyed, submitted to the embrace and then stared at her mother fixedly, as if her reason had deserted her. Frightened and grief-stricken, Josephine called Dr. Corvisart and implored him to save her daughter. The celebrated physician concluded that only time and a change of scene could cure Hortense.

Louis returned to Holland alone, and Josephine took her daughter and grandson back to Malmaison. But despite the tenderest care, Hortense remained in her dazed condition, pale, motionless for hours, ferociously silent. Every day, at the hour her little son had died, she was shaken by a fit of weeping, would call out her child's name as if he were there, and talk about him to the Empress. "Only a little while ago he was here with me," she said. "I held him here on my knee." Then she would sink again into her unnatural silence.

At Dr. Corvisart's advice, the Empress allowed Hortense to visit the Pyrenees, while she herself took on the care of Napoleon Louis. It was a beneficial move, for not long afterward she received word at Saint-Cloud that her daughter was well again, and had recovered from the stupor of her bereavement.

Then came triumphant news of the victory at Friedland and the truce with Russia. Toward the end of June, Napoleon had met the young Czar Alexander at Tilsit and a preliminary peace was being drawn up. He wrote that he would soon return to Paris.

Meanwhile, by an Imperial decree, the marriage of Jérôme Bonaparte with the American, Eleanor Patterson, had been annulled; and a few days after the Emperor's return to Paris the German princes of the Confederation of the Rhine arrived in France to attend the marriage of Princess Catherine of Württemberg and Jérôme Bonaparte. Napoleon had made Jérôme King of Westphalia, by the terms of the Treaty of Tilsit, signed in July, 1807.

Hortense returned to France and was at Saint-Cloud on August 27 for the Emperor's affectionate greeting. He pretended to tease and reprove her for having run off to the mountains and abandoning her mother and son.

Napoleon seemed to be in a good humor, and ready to talk about the Prussian and Polish campaigns and his meeting with Czar Alexander at Tilsit. "He's a charming young man," said Napoleon, "I like him very much. As for the Queen of Prussia, she is beautiful and kindly, but a little affected." Then, turning toward the Empress, he added, "She's not the equal of my Josephine."

Thereupon he gave his wife a kiss, whispered some gay, loving words in her ear, and, realizing that Hortense might have overheard, burst out laughing. "I've never known a cruel woman," he said.

"That's because you've made overtures only to compliant women," Hortense retorted.

He stared at her, laughed again, and pinched her ear so hard she cried out.

"Do you hear how your daughter treats me?" he said to Josephine. "She thinks I've always been old!"

In the autumn, the court followed the Emperor to Fontainebleau where life was a round of hunting parties, concerts, and balls. Hortense, pregnant again, did not travel by road with the others, but took a boat up the river. She dreaded returning to Holland and kept postponing it; but one day she received a command from her husband: She must send little Napoleon Louis back to him at The Hague.

Throughout the following months the rumor was circulated that Napoleon was about to divorce Josephine. Backed by Fouché, Caroline and her husband Prince Murat were again secretly scheming to bring it about, but the Emperor seemed to be unaware of the rumors and intrigues. Hortense, however, had a conversation with her stepfather about this time, in which he revealed matters that lay heavily on his mind.

Hortense had sought him out to report Louis's command that their child be sent back to Holland.

Napoleon frowned when he heard her. "Your child is frail and delicate," he said. "He is the only male child in the family. If he goes back to Holland he will die as his elder brother did, and all France will compel me to divorce your mother. She has no confidence in my brothers. . . . Eugène does not bear my name. After me, there would be complete anarchy. A son of mine could bring harmony, and if I have not divorced your mother it is only because of my affection for her, for it is the avowed wish of all France."

Toward the end of the sojourn at Fontainebleau that autumn, Fouché had a private talk with the Empress.

"We must not fool ourselves, Madame," he said to her. "Public opinion is anxious about the succession. All France demands that the Emperor repudiate you. Sooner or later the Emperor will have to bring himself to it."

Josephine, utterly stricken, told her most devoted ladies in waiting about this conversation, and that Fouché had urged her to take the initiative. At Madame de Rémusat's advice, Josephine replied negatively to Fouché: She refused to take any step. She said nothing of all this to the Emperor, who reproached her later for her silence and declared that Fouché had acted without his authority. Napoleon asked her, nevertheless, how she felt about it, and Josephine realized that he suffered at the idea of breaking up their marriage bond.

She replied in a sad, calm voice: "Sire, you will decide my fate. When you command me to leave the Tuileries, I shall obey. But I cannot be the first to demand a parting from you. I should be afraid of bringing misfortune upon us both if, of my own free will, I were to cut off my life from yours."

Deeply affected, Napoleon withdrew. From then on, torn in two directions, he was alternately very irritable and very tender with his wife. "My poor dear Josephine, I could never leave you," he told her one night, his face bathed in tears.

The Empress passed unceasingly from fear to hope, and from hope to despair.

The Iberian peninsula, meanwhile, was giving trouble, and that winter Napoleon had sent an army under Junot to occupy Portugal. After some hard fighting at Abrantès, the country was pacified and the royal family fled to Brazil. The following spring, however, Spain was so troublesome that Napoleon realized he must drive out the Bourbons and give the crown to his brother Joseph. Murat was dispatched as commander in chief of the French armies on the peninsula, and Napoleon set out for Bayonne.

A new rumor spread, that Napoleon intended to marry the Grand Duchess Catherine of Russia.

A few days before his departure for Bayonne, Hortense had bade him farewell. Her pregnancy was very apparent now that a third child would soon be born.

"Oh, it hurts me to see you like this!" Napoleon exclaimed. "How I would love your mother if she were in your condition!"

Josephine joined the Emperor at Marrac, not far from Bayonne. The months that followed were like the weather, woven of blue and gold. Josephine was happy even though she had to overlook a few infidelities, for never had Napoleon seemed more in love with her. He spent all his leisure hours with her, and was his old gay self again, amusing her, playing pranks. It was like another honeymoon. Sometimes, like children, they ran together on the beach, he pursuing her and pushing her into the water, laughing loudly. Once he threw her slippers into the sea, and she had to return barefooted in the carriage.

In April, news reached them of the birth of Hortense's third son, Louis Napoleon. The Emperor joyfully ordered "all the guns on the Spanish border to salute the event with a salvo."

They returned to Fontainebleau at the end of August. The

Emperor could not stay, for troubles were brewing everywhere, requiring his presence at the head of the armies. He set off first for Erfurth, for another conference with the Czar, and then for Spain, which had risen in revolt against Joseph and his tottering throne. On January 23, 1809, he was again in Paris; but on April 13, he left France once more: Austria had thrown her armies against Italy, Dalmatia, Bavaria.

Napoleon took Josephine to Strasbourg where she remained until the latter part of July. Reassured by the victories of Raab and Wagram, she went to Plombières, and in mid-August returned to Malmaison. There Hortense joined her in October.

The Queen of Holland found her mother almost ill with apprehension. Napoleon had written her often enough during the German campaign—but what curt letters! Eugène's military successes at Raab and at Wagram had given rise in the army to talk that irritated Napoleon. After the armistice of Znaïm a German student had tried to assassinate the Emperor, and the attempt threw the French generals into an uproar. If Napoleon had been slain, who would have succeeded him? They decided on Eugène as the most logical and desirable successor. When he learned their choice, the Emperor was no longer reluctant to obtain a divorce: "It is indispensable. Public opinion is deranged."

Napoleon had sent for Countess Walewska in Vienna, and for three months they lived openly together at Schoenbrunn. In Vienna Marie Walewska was referred to as the Emperor's Polish wife, and there was a rumor that she was pregnant.

Finally, in November, as if to remove Josephine's last illusion, Napoleon sent her the following curt note: "My dear, I am leaving in an hour. I shall be at Fontainebleau from the twenty-sixth to the twenty-seventh. You may go there with a few ladies."

After writing those lines, Napoleon ordered an architect of the palace at Saint-Cloud to wall up the doors between his rooms and those of the Empress.

Perhaps he was afraid of his own heart. In any case, from the very first day of his return, he behaved coldly and distantly toward Josephine. There were no more private talks, no more opportunities for a reconciliation. They were never left alone. He no longer rode out in his carriage with her, taking instead his sister Pauline, with whom he spent his evenings. And Josephine learned that at Pauline's house he had again encountered a woman he had known in Piedmont, Madame de Mathis, whom Hortense described as "a rather fat blonde." This was a stormy affair and soon over.

Everyone at court spied upon Josephine, and knowing that her disgrace was not far off, the members of her entourage forgot the marks of respect due her. The Empress continued to smile, however, and addressed only kind words to everyone. They were indifferent to her favors. Many of them even remained seated in her presence, and chatted and laughed with the chamberlains. Some of them whispered, with unmistakable expressions of irony or pity on their faces.

# 6

## The Divorce

ON THE EVENING OF November 30, 1809, the Emperor dined
alone with the Empress. From time to time he addressed
a remark to the chamberlain who was supervising the service.
Josephine, barely holding back her tears, did not touch her
food and remained silent. Coffee was served in the little drawing room, and Napoleon himself took his cup from a footman.
After filling it with coffee, he indicated that he wished to be
left alone with the Empress.

Bausset, the chamberlain, was stationed outside the door
to supervise the footmen clearing away the dinner table. He
heard Josephine's voice raised in a scream, and suddenly the
door opened and Napoleon appeared. "Come in, Bausset," he
said. "I shall need your help."

Josephine was lying prostrate on the floor, where she had
fallen in an apparent swoon. She was conscious, however, and
uttering heart-rending little moans.

"No, I cannot survive it," she said sobbingly, and then lay
quiet, with her eyes closed, her face very pale.

"She must be carried to her room," Napoleon said, "and
given the care she needs— No, by the inner stairway!"

They carried her together, Napoleon holding her legs, and
a palace guard going ahead with a candlestick. They descended
the very narrow stairway that led to Josephine's apartment

with great difficulty. Bausset was panting from the effort, and became entangled with his sword, bumping the Empress. She opened her eyes and murmured, "You're hurting me."

After entrusting Josephine to her personal maids, Napoleon called for Dr. Corvisart. Bausset had never seen his master so upset. The physician arrived to find the Emperor weeping.

"I have had to do violence to my heart," Napoleon said. "Divorce has become a rigorous duty. I am all the more affected because of Josephine's scene . . . only three days ago . . . she must have known from Hortense . . . that I was resolved to part with her. . . . I pity her with all my soul . . ."

He could barely speak, so choked was his voice. The words came out jerkily. "I thought she had more character . . . I was not prepared for such an outburst of grief."

Reassured by Corvisart, he went upstairs to his own rooms where he presently received Hortense. Afraid of giving way to his emotions again, his words and manner were curt:

"You have seen your mother. What did she tell you? My decision is final. It is irrevocable. All France demands the divorce. . . . Nothing will make me waver now, neither prayers nor tears. . . ." He paused, then with irritation: "I expect to be obeyed."

"Sire," Hortense replied in a calm and humble tone, "you are the master. You will be opposed by no one. Since your happiness demands it, that is enough. We know how to sacrifice ourselves. Do not be surprised at my mother's tears. You should rather have been surprised if, after a union of thirteen years, she had shed no tears. But she will submit with good grace, I am sure, and we will all go away, taking with us the memory of your kindnesses."

Napoleon could no longer control his growing emotion. As Hortense, the child of Josephine whom he had brought up as his own, pronounced these dignified and simple words, his expression changed. In a voice choked with sobs, he exclaimed:

"What! You will leave me? You will abandon me? You no longer love me?"

His eyes were wet with tears as he implored Hortense to remain, with Eugène, at his side. The welfare of the State, alone, forced him to part from Josephine. Josephine would always remain his love, his best, his only. . . .

Touched at his grief which seemed to be sincere, Hortense dropped all pride and wept in her turn.

"Have courage, Sire. We shall need it to be your children no more."

Napoleon refused to listen, and insisted on keeping Eugène and Hortense near him.

"Sire," she said, recovering her poise, "my duty is to my mother. She will need me. We cannot live near you any more. It is a sacrifice required of us, and we will carry it out."

The next day and all the following days, Josephine, despite her affliction, had to appear in public to perform her duties as sovereign as in the past, with the same grace, the same gestures, the same tone of voice, "at the same time imposing and charming."

Eugène arrived on the fifth of December and went at once to Napoleon's rooms. Hortense waited for him, with her mother. A little while afterward Napoleon came down the inner stairway with Eugène.

Josephine had not seen her son since his marriage to the Princess Augusta of Bavaria. How happy she had been, then! The Emperor divined her thoughts and was so moved that he was on the point of revoking his orders. Eugène and Hortense dissuaded him: It was too late. The Empress could no longer be happy with him. They must separate.

At that moment, Josephine declared she knew how to accept her fate. She wanted only that her son's future be assured, and asked that he be given the Kingdom of Italy.

Eugène interrupted her with a gesture. No, no! No bargaining! The sacrifice must be accepted without thought of the consequences.

"That's the Eugène I know," said the Emperor. "And he is right to believe in my affection."

He repeated what he had already told Hortense: The Empress should keep her position; he would always take care of her with tenderness.

Eugène insisted on a complete separation. "Our situation would be false. Our family would be open to attack. Even your enemies could harm you by pretending to be our friends, and you would be led to unjustified distrust of us."

Napoleon still insisted. "Eugène," he said gravely, "if I have been of any use to you, and if I have at all taken the place of a father, do not abandon me. I need you. Your sister cannot leave me. Your mother does not wish to . . ."

Then he added, more persuasively: "Stay, if you do not want it to be said, 'The Empress was sent away; she deserved it perhaps.' If she remains near me, then surely her role is fine enough, to keep her rank, her dignities—to prove that this is entirely a political separation, one that she wished, too. Will she not be held in even greater esteem by the nation for which she sacrifices herself?"

On December 15, 1809, at nine o'clock in the evening, the Imperial family assembled at the Tuileries. In the Throne Room, gathered round the Emperor and Empress and *Madame Mère*, were Louis, Jérôme, Murat, Eugène, Hortense, Catherine, Pauline, and Caroline.

Addressing himself to the Grand Chancellor Cambacérès, the Emperor read aloud in a firm voice a speech that was marked throughout with affection and regret. After announcing his resolve, which he had taken with the Empress, he added:

"God knows how much this resolution has cost my heart.

But there is no sacrifice that is beyond my courage when it is demonstrably for the good of France.

"I must add that, far from ever having reason to complain, I have, on the contrary, had reason only to congratulate myself for the tenderness and affection of my beloved wife. She has embellished thirteen years of my life; the memory will always be engraved in my heart. She was crowned by my hand. I desire that she preserve the rank and title of Empress, but above all that she never doubt my affection and always consider me her best and dearest friend."

When he came to the words, "she has embellished thirteen years of my life," he could not hide his emotion. As he sat down, he turned his eyes toward Josephine with an expression that was charged with tenderness.

Dressed in a very simple, white dress, without ornament, the Empress then stood up to reply, pale and trembling a little. The eyes of Louis, Pauline, Caroline, and Murat were fixed upon her with expressions of triumph and hate. In order not to sweeten their victory further, she forced herself to remain calm, as she read in her sweetly musical voice the following declaration:

"With the permission of our august and beloved spouse, I must declare that, having no hope of bearing children who could satisfy his political needs and the interests of France, it pleases me to give him the greatest proof of attachment and devotion that has ever been given on earth ..."

Josephine, half-fainting, had to stop. She made an effort to go on, but her tears prevented it. With a convulsive gesture she thrust the paper at the secretary of state, Regnaud de Saint-Jean-d'Angély, who finished the reading.

At its completion, Grand Chancellor Cambacérès drew up the report of the divorce proceedings and handed the pen to the Emperor, the Empress, *Madame Mère*, and all the kings and queens, princes and princesses. When the entire Imperial family had signed, the Emperor kissed the Empress, took her by the hand, and led her to her rooms.

The next day the dissolution of "the marriage contracted between the Emperor Napoleon and the Empress Josephine" was proclaimed in the Senate. The same proclamation fixed at two million francs the "widow's dower." To this the Emperor, by special decree, added an annual allowance of one million francs to be drawn from the Crown Treasury and the properties of the Elysée Palace, Malmaison, and the domain of Navarre.

# Part IV

## THE EMPRESS IN RETIREMENT
### (1809-1814)

ЛЛЛЛЛЛЛЛЛЛЛЛЛЛЛЛЛЛЛЛЛЛЛЛЛ

# 1

## *An Enduring Love*

Méneval, come with me," the Emperor said to his secretary. "We are going to Malmaison to visit the Empress."

Josephine, at the sight of Napoleon, stood up suddenly and threw herself upon his breast, sobbing. He held her close, kissing her eyes, as if to stop the flow of tears, and then gently released her.

This scene, re-enacted many times during the months and years that followed, first occurred on a rainy day not long after the divorce. The Empress Josephine, in retirement at Malmaison, was receiving her first visitors.

The rain had been pouring down when Josephine drove away from the Tuileries, with Eugène and Hortense beside her in the court carriage, *Opale*, that was to convey her to Malmaison. At first they remained silent. Nothing could be heard except the pattering of raindrops on the carriage windows, the tinkle of harness bells, the thud of the horses' hoofs, and the rumbling of the wheels, to which was occasionally added the shrieks of a parakeet whose cage was on top of a stack of boxes in a carriage that trailed them.

Josephine broke her silence only once to say to Hortense, "If he is happy, I shall not repent," and then lapsed again into a sad revery.

It was at Malmaison, where she and Napoleon had lived so long and happily together, that Josephine felt her solitude most keenly.

It was still raining the next day when Audenarde, whom the Emperor had sent for news, found her in tears. Shortly afterward she received some lady visitors, friends who had remained faithful to her: the Duchesse de Bassano, the Duchesse de Rovigo (formerly Madame Savary), the Duchesse d' Elchingen (formerly Madame Ney), the Duchesse de Raguse, the Comtesse de Montalivet, the Comtesse de Ségur, the Comtesse de Luçay, and, oddly enough, the Comtesse Duchatel.

To hide the ravages of tears, she wore a wide-brimmed white hat that shaded her eyes. Laure Junot, now the Duchesse d'Abrantès, came late and found the Empress sitting in her drawing room beside the fireplace. Above it hung a painting by Girodet representing the Generals Kléber, Hoche, and Marceau being welcomed to the Elysian Fields by the Scottish bard Ossian.

Josephine received her visitors with her usual graciousness. Her lips smiled, but occasionally the tears that she tried to hold back escaped and rolled down her cheeks. When she saw Laure, she held out her hand and said, "I almost want to kiss you. You have come on a day of mourning!"

A letter from the Emperor, who had established himself at the Trianon, was brought to her by a footman. She had just finished reading it when the Emperor himself arrived. He did not kiss her, and hardly entered the room, but took her by the hand and walked up and down with her in front of the château. After exchanging a few words they both fell silent. Josephine's strength soon failed, and they sat down on a nearby bench. They both seemed too moved to speak.

Immediately upon his return to the Trianon, the Emperor wrote her a short but affectionate letter:

Eight o'clock in the evening

My dear,

I found you today more lacking in strength than you should be. You have shown courage; you must find courage to sustain yourself. Do not give way to a dreary melancholy. If you are attached to me, if you love me, you must be strong. You cannot doubt my constant and tender affection, and you little know the feelings I have for you if you suppose that I can be happy when you are not happy, and content when you are not at peace with yourself.

Adieu, my dear, sleep well. Know that I wish it.

Madame de Rémusat urged Josephine to go out, to relax her mind by exerting her body. Josephine let herself be advised and questioned, agreed to everything without resisting, saying: "It seems to me that I am dead and that nothing is left except a vague feeling that I am no more."

For a week, Napoleon lived at the Trianon in unusual idleness. Every day he wrote to Josephine, pitying her solitude, and declaring that he missed her greatly. On Christmas Day he invited her and Hortense to dine with him at the Trianon. He seated himself opposite her at the table, as usual, and nothing seemed changed. But, despite the presence of Caroline, the dinner passed in almost complete silence. From time to time the Emperor wiped his eyes with his fingers. Josephine looked as if she were about to faint.

The next day Napoleon returned to Paris. As long as he had remained at the Trianon, Josephine had not felt the final break. But now that he had returned to the Tuileries, where they had lived together for ten years, she felt her downfall keenly. Napoleon, told of this by her son, again wrote affectionately: "Eugène has told me that you were very sad yesterday. That's not good, my dear. It's contrary to what you promised me. I was very vexed at seeing the Tuileries again. This great palace seemed empty, and I felt isolated . . ."

Time dragged on at Malmaison. The Emperor gradually wrote to her less frequently and came to see her even more rarely. Josephine and Hortense often sat in a little room over-looking the highway. Every time there was a hunt in the forest of Saint-Germain, Josephine watched at the window for the arrival of the Emperor's carriage, and would not leave it until she had seen him depart.

Napoleon, worried about her persisting melancholy, wrote to her reprovingly: "I should like very much to visit you at Malmaison, but you will have to be strong and calm. This morning the footman told me he had seen you weeping. I am going to dine alone. Adieu, my dear."

He finally paid the promised visit. Afterward, in a letter dated January 7, 1810, he wrote to tell her he was "working" for her with Estève, his treasurer: "I have allotted 100,000 francs ... for the extra expenses at Malmaison. So now you can plant all the flowers you like; you may use this sum as you wish."

To this gift the Emperor added other bounties: Josephine received 200,000 francs for the purchase of the Bois-Préau property, and for the purchase of linen and silver an additional 600,000 francs.

The Emperor "worked" for her in other ways.

"Have you seen the Empress?" he would casually ask some-one at the Tuileries. This was all it took to crowd the road to Malmaison with carriages. Very soon, after being neglected and abandoned by most of the ladies and courtiers of the palace, Josephine was once more surrounded by a throng of visitors, who wearied her with their compliments and flatteries.

These visitors were soon followed by a succession of mon-archs, princes, and royalty. In their turn, the King and Queen of Bavaria, the King of Württemberg, the King of Saxony came to bow before her.

But nothing could comfort Josephine's heart. Her nights were disturbed by fears and regrets. She was homesick for Paris and longed for her life there. Would the Emperor grant this favor? According to gossip, he was thinking of banishing her from France. It was said he would exile her when a new Empress reigned at the Tuileries, and she knew that a marriage with the Austrian Archduchess Marie Louise was being arranged. Napoleon wrote to her, after Eugène, at her request, had made some discreet inquiries:

"I learn that you are grieving. That's not good. You have no faith in me to let yourself be hurt by every rumor that is being circulated. That is not knowing me, Josephine . . ."

Three days later he again wrote: "I told Eugène that you apparently prefer to listen to the gossips of a big city than to what I tell you; that people must stop spreading tales that hurt you. I have had your effects transferred to the Elysée Palace. You will come at once to Paris."

Josephine wasted no time, and that very night she slept at the Elysée. But there she soon felt more imprisoned and abandoned than at Malmaison. The Emperor's life was full of theater parties, balls, and private theatricals, on top of matters of state. He had time for only occasional brief visits with Josephine. All around her in Paris there was movement, and Josephine had to watch it from her windows. She had time to reflect upon the marriage that was soon to take place, and to wonder about the young Archduchess Marie Louise, who would become Napoleon's wife on April 1.

When the date was set for the future Empress's departure from Vienna, Josephine left Paris and returned to Malmaison.

She did not stay there long, for the Emperor decided she would be too near Paris for the wedding ceremonies. He issued a command that she withdraw to the château of Navarre near Evreux for the month of April.

The château of Navarre was a great, square building with a truncated dome, set between two wooded slopes on a marshy plain. It was surrounded by rivers, waterfalls, and ponds, and proved to be unbearably humid and cold. An odor of mildew filled every room, the windows were ill-fitting, the woodwork crumbling, and it was only partially furnished. There was no way to heat the great circular drawing room, and the walls oozed dampness and decay.

The ladies and gentlemen of Josephine's retinue muttered about being left at this time of year in an isolated château three stagecoach posts from Paris! And there were some defections. The "faithful" Madame de Rémusat had not accompanied her mistress at all, apparently feeling she performed her duty better by writing a letter asking for news! The steward of the castle sent to Paris for additional furniture; and when the carriage-loads of goods arrived they were pillaged and fought over by members of Josephine's household.

As soon as Josephine learned that Napoleon and his bride, the Empress Marie Louise, were spending their honeymoon in the château of Compiègne, she wrote a formal letter to him, asking permission to return to Malmaison. Although the request was worded ceremoniously, it contained discreet allusions to the past calculated to arouse pity in the Emperor:

Navarre, April 19, 1810

Sire,

I have received, through my son, the assurance that Your Majesty will consent to my return to Malmaison, and likewise graciously accord me the advances I requested for rendering the château of Navarre habitable.

This double favor, Sire, dispels in great part the anxieties and fears that Your Majesty's long silence had inspired. I was afraid I had been entirely banished from your memory: I see that I am not. I am therefore less unhappy today; indeed, I am as happy as it is possible for me to be from now on.

At the end of the month I shall go to Malmaison, since Your Majesty does not oppose it. . . . I shall depart soon thereafter to take the waters. But while I am at Malmaison, Your Majesty may rest assured that I shall live as if I were a thousand leagues from Paris. I have made a great sacrifice, Sire, and each day I feel more and more the extent of it. However, this sacrifice shall be, as it should be, complete, on my part. Your Majesty's happiness shall not be troubled by any expression of my regrets.

I shall always pray for Your Majesty's happiness; perhaps I shall even pray that I may see Your Majesty again; but Your Majesty may rest assured that I shall always respect the new situation; I shall respect it in silence. Confident of the sentiments Your Majesty entertained for me in former times, I shall not provoke any new proof; I shall await everything from his justice and his heart. . . .

The Emperor replied immediately, using a tender and familiar tone: "My dear, I received your letter of April 19; it is written in bad style. I am still the same; men of my kind never change. . . . I see with pleasure that you will go to Malmaison and are content with it. My content will be in having news of you and giving you mine. I shall say no more until you have compared this letter with yours; and after that I shall let you judge which of us is the better and kinder friend, you or I."

How well Josephine knew the Emperor! She had succeeded in stirring his pity, awakening his tenderness, obliging him to think about her. Despite his new marriage, Napoleon had written to her in his usual intimate way. Josephine had wanted to make him deny the intentions ascribed to him by rumor: that to please the new Empress he was considering making Josephine only the Duchesse de Navarre, relegating her to the Duchy of Berg! His letter reassured her, and in her joy and gratitude she immediately wrote back to him in the same intimate style, calculated to move him again and even more profoundly:

"A thousand, thousand tender thanks for not having forgotten me! My son has just handed me your letter. With what ardor I have read it! And yet I read it slowly, for not a word in it does not make me weep; but they were very sweet tears! I found my heart whole again, and it will always be that way.

There are some feelings that are life itself and can end only with life.

"I have written you only once since leaving Malmaison, but how many times have I wanted to write to you! But I realized the reasons for your silence and was afraid to bother you with a letter. Yours has been a balm for me. Be happy, as happy as you deserve to be! I say it with my whole heart. You have just given me my share of happiness, and a poignant one. Nothing is worth more to me than a mark of your remembrance.

"Adieu, my dear, I thank you as tenderly as I shall always love you."

# 2

## The Anguish of Exile

IN MAY, Josephine returned to Malmaison. The Emperor, who was reviewing his fleet at Antwerp, wrote her from there, authorizing her to spend the summer at Aix-en-Savoie:

"I heartily approve of your taking the waters at Aix," he declared. "I want very much to see you, and if you are still at Malmaison at the end of the month, I will pay you a visit. I count on being at Saint-Cloud on the thirtieth.... Let me know under what name you will travel. My feelings for you will last as long as I do. You do me an injustice if you doubt it."

At Malmaison Josephine took up her old habits, happy to be with her flowers again and her dearest memories. She had forbidden any piece of furniture to be moved in the rooms formerly occupied by the Emperor. Instead of using his apartment, she preferred to confine herself to her old quarters on the second floor. A glance into his rooms showed a history book open on the desk, the pen still dark with ink, the globe still bearing the marks of his blue pencil. One would have said that Napoleon had just stepped out for a few minutes.

Josephine herself dusted his "relics." Few people were authorized to enter his bedroom, which also looked as if it were still in use. The Roman bed still waited for him, his weapons still hung on the wall, and some of his clothing was scattered about on the chairs ...

Despite her objections and refusals, Hortense had finally been obliged to rejoin her husband in Holland. But she had left behind her third child, Louis Napoleon, who would one day rule France as Napoleon III. Nicknamed *Monsieur Oui-Oui*, her little grandson was Josephine's favorite and was often brought by his nurse to Malmaison. He was one of Josephine's greatest solaces in exile.

The Emperor and the Empress Marie Louise returned to Saint-Cloud at the beginning of June, and Josephine waited for the promised visit. It took place on the thirteenth, and Josephine reported on it in a letter to Hortense:

"Yesterday was a day of happiness: The Emperor came to see me. His presence made me happy even though it renewed my grief.... These are the kinds of emotions we should like to feel often. All the time he was with me I had enough courage to hold back tears that were ready to fall. But when he had left I was very unhappy. He was kind and pleasant to me as usual, and I hope he read in my heart all the tenderness and devotion I have for him."

Two days after this, traveling under the name of Comtesse d'Arberg, she left for Aix, accompanied by Mesdames d'Audenarde and de Rémusat, Mademoiselle de Mackau, and Messieurs de Turpin and de Pourtalès.

There were few people at Aix when the Empress Josephine arrived; but soon, from everywhere, crowds of the curious flocked to see her and beg favors of her, just as in the time of her power.

From the day of her arrival, she adopted and followed a modest, orderly way of life. In the mornings, after taking the waters by bath and shower, she was borne home in a sedan chair. She then rested in bed until luncheon, and in the afternoon she worked at her tapestries with her ladies in waiting, who read aloud plays or novels. She would then be dressed for dinner, and after dinner she took a carriage ride. At nine o'clock the carriage returned to the "palace" for "the Empress's amusements."

Shortly after her arrival in Aix, Josephine heard disturbing news from Holland. Hortense, after a series of quarrels with Louis, had left him and gone to Plombières. Josephine, knowing that her daughter was very ill, implored her to come to Aix:

"Let me see you, my dear daughter. Alone, abandoned, far from my own in the midst of strangers, you can imagine how sad I am and how much I need your presence."

Her anguish redoubled when she learned of Louis's abdication, and his flight from Holland, leaving behind his son Napoleon Louis, Grand-Duc de Berg, as the young pretender to a toppling throne. It was the Emperor himself who announced the bad news to her: "The King of Holland has abdicated. . . . He has left Amsterdam, abandoning the Grand-Duc de Berg. I have annexed Holland to France; but this act has the happy feature of emancipating the Queen, and that unfortunate girl will come to Paris with her son, the Grand-Duc de Berg; that will make her perfectly happy."

Reassured as to the destiny Napoleon reserved for Hortense and the one he was preparing for little Napoleon Louis, Josephine looked forward to her daughter's early arrival. While waiting, she toured Savoy with her "court," to which the amiable Charles de Flahaut had just attached himself. In crossing Lake Bourget after a visit to the ancient Abbey of Hautecombe, her boat was caught in a storm and nearly wrecked. In reply to her letter describing this near-catastrophe, the Emperor wrote teasingly from the Trianon: "I was troubled to read of the danger you ran. For an inhabitant of the ocean isles to die in a lake would have been a fatality!"

Hortense arrived the day after this event, pale, thin, and downcast, showing the ravages of her "lung trouble" and her misfortunes. She was cheered when she heard that her son had been brought from Amsterdam and was with the Emperor at Saint-Cloud. Gradually her gaiety returned in the atmosphere of affection with which the Empress surrounded her, and under the charming attentions of Charles de Flahaut.

A few days after Flahaut's departure for Paris, Josephine left Hortense at Aix and went to Geneva. It was too late in the season to go to Milan, where Eugène was.

Josephine was at Sécheron, outside Geneva, when she heard of the pregnancy of Marie Louise. She at once wrote to the Emperor, who confirmed the news: "My dear," he wrote, "the Empress is, in effect, four months pregnant. She is in good health and very attached to me."

The tone of this note disquieted Josephine. She anticipated with dread being banished from France, and felt saddened by her equivocal position. When Hortense rejoined her, she related the rumors she had heard. It was being said that Marie Louise was very disturbed by the affection Napoleon had for his first wife. Her pride as an Austrian archduchess, and as a young bride, was wounded by the attentions her husband still paid to the fallen Empress, a woman of no lineage and old enough to seek oblivion.

Josephine had heard these same rumors from Eugène and Madame de Rémusat. The Viceroy of Italy had advised his mother to prolong her stay in Geneva; her presence in Paris or too near Paris would only further offend the Empress Marie Louise. Madame de Rémusat likewise insisted upon the necessity of keeping distance between the two empresses.

When he had remarried, the Emperor was confident that he could easily bring the two women together, but now he witnessed a growing rivalry that disturbed him. In trying to please them both, he had made them both jealous. Marie Louise, soon to become a mother, was defending her newly acquired rights; Josephine was trying to recapture those she had enjoyed for thirteen years. The best thing was to persuade Josephine to remain outside France.

But Napoleon's sensitivity and his persisting tenderness for Josephine made it impossible for him to behave cruelly toward

her. He shrank from imposing his will on her by command.
Perhaps it would be better to suggest a voluntary exile, only a
temporary one, of course. Madame de Rémusat was summoned to Paris and charged with the mission.

In a long letter couched in flowery language, decorated with
flattering words, Josephine's confidante gave her advice that
was "dictated by the Emperor's attachment to her." To his
great regret, the Emperor has been unable to establish cordial
relations between the two empresses. Perhaps it was too soon
to hope for a reconciliation. The imagination of Marie Louise
was quick to take offense: She had one day burst into tears
when the Emperor had suggested that she accompany him on
a visit to Malmaison. This disposition to jealousy would be
weakened in time, no doubt. But meanwhile they must act
with extra prudence because the young Empress was pregnant.
And Josephine must consider how untenable her position
would be in Paris during the festivities that would follow such
an impatiently awaited birth! "What could the Emperor do?"
Madame de Rémusat asked. "He must act circumspectly because of his wife's condition, and yet he is still disturbed by
the memory of the affection he holds for you. He would suffer,
as you, too, would suffer. You could not endure so much rejoicing without a pang, while you would no doubt be forgotten
by a whole nation, or else the object of pity for a few who side
with you against the Emperor. Little by little your situation
would become so painful that only a complete exile could cure
it. You would have to leave Paris. Malmaison and even
Navarre would be too near.... Then, forced to go away, you
would seem to be fleeing from or obeying a command, and
would lose all the prestige that could be yours, if you took the
initiative courageously."

Madame de Rémusat reported that all her observations were
the result of an interview with Duroc, the grand marshal of
the palace, and not with the Emperor. She herself agreed with
Duroc that Josephine should make this additional sacrifice.

Yes, the Empress Josephine's dignity demanded that instead of waiting for the force of events, she should forestall them by taking a brave step. "In sparing the Emperor this embarrassment, from which, because of his affection for you, there is no issue for him, you will win new claim to his esteem. Moreover," she suggested insidiously, "you will perhaps find in a more prolonged voyage pleasures that you cannot now foresee." She vaunted the pleasures of Milan, Florence, and Rome in the winter, which would soon give way to "the season when you can live at Navarre," whose château would require Josephine's presence to advise in matters of rebuilding and redecoration.

Madame de Rémusat ended piously with the hope that "Time, the great Restorer, will settle all difficulties, and your noble conduct will assure you the gratitude of an entire nation."

Josephine knew that Duroc did not like her, and she mistrusted Madame de Rémusat. What was she to conclude from this interminable letter of Madame de Rémusat, which despite its ceremonious tone seemed to contain threats of a perpetual banishment?

She entrusted Hortense, who was about to return to Paris, with a letter to the Emperor.

The court was at Fontainebleau, and Hortense went there at once to deliver her mother's letter. Napoleon wanted Josephine to have a long stay with her son in Milan. "I must think of my wife's happiness," he added. "Things have not turned out as I hoped. Marie Louise is dismayed at the privileges your mother enjoys and the influence she is known to exercise over me." After a moment's silence, he continued more gently: "No matter what happens, I will never put restraints on the Empress Josephine. I will always remember the sacrifice she made for me. If she wants to establish herself in Rome, I will name her ruler of the city. In Brussels, she could hold an even more superb court. . . . Near her son and grandchildren in

Milan she will be still better off, and more comfortable. But write her that if she prefers to live at Malmaison, I will not oppose it."

A few days later, Napoleon announced the official separation of Hortense and Louis, and gave his stepdaughter the title of Duchesse de Saint-Leu.

To "divert her thoughts" Josephine left for Bern, and made another tour of Switzerland, visiting Thoun, Interlaken, Lausanne, Ferney, Coppet—where she refused to see Madame de Staël—and purchased the estate of Prégny-la-Tour near Petit-Sacconex. In Geneva, she received a letter from the Emperor that put an end to her anxieties.

"Visit your son this winter," he wrote, "and return to take the waters at Aix next year; or else spend the spring at Navarre. I should advise you to go to Navarre immediately if I did not fear you would be bored there. My opinion is that you cannot, with propriety, spend the winter anywhere but in Milan or Navarre. After that, I approve of anything you may do, for I do not want to hinder you in anything. Good-by, my dear. The Empress is four months pregnant. Be happy, don't be angry, and never doubt my affection."

When it became known that the Emperor had authorized Josephine to return to France there was an outburst of joy from her entourage. On November 1, 1810, they set out for Malmaison, where Josephine wanted to spend a few days before going on to Navarre. Her return was "an event." Everyone who was discontented and repelled by the arrogant new Empress, everyone who missed the first Empress, all the former Jacobins and the nobles of the Faubourg Saint-Germain, the tradesmen who found Marie Louise stingy and inclined to haggle—all of them invaded Josephine's little château.

At Fontainebleau everything was ceremonious and cold, the receptions, theatricals, and other entertainments were cramped and stiff. At Malmaison everything was easy and affluent; good humor was as important as dignity. And even though no favors could be granted, people flocked to Malmaison, despite the distance from Paris.

Josephine's new court consisted of the Comtesse d'Arberg, her lady in waiting and stewardess of the household; Mesdames de Rémusat, de Ségur, de Viel-Castel, de Colbert, de Serrant, de Turenne, de Lastic, d'Audenarde—a Creole; the young Mesdemoiselles de Mackau, de Castellane, and Georgette Ducrest, so pretty and charming that she was a little envied; and Madame Gazzani, Josephine's "reader." It was a gay and charming society, rendered even more so when Hortense joined it. To avoid rivalry in dress, the former sovereign decreed a kind of uniform of dark green.

Josephine's affable, charming "gentleman in waiting," Monsieur de Beaumont, was liked by everyone, but the same could not be said of her four chamberlains and her four equerries: The ineptness of the Marquis de Viel-Castel seemed excessive; the insolence of Monsieur de Monaco was equaled only by the rudeness of Monsieur de Montlivault; the Comte de Pourtalès's stiff respectability caused smirks. The only other agreeable gentleman in the retinue was the amateur painter, Monsieur de Turpin-Crissé, whose paintings Josephine bought.

In the afternoons there were strolls in the park to visit the hothouse or to feed the golden pheasants, the guinea fowl, and the other rare birds in the aviary. In the evenings they took strolls, or a concert was given while the Empress played whist or solitaire.

Time passed so gently and pleasantly that Josephine kept postponing her departure for Navarre. The Emperor, on the point of leaving Fontainebleau for the Tuileries, sent his Grand Chancellor to Malmaison: Josephine must resign herself to leaving.

Before her departure, Josephine wrote to Eugène, telling him her plans:

"It seems that the Empress Marie Louise has no desire

whatsoever to see me. On that point, we are in perfect accord, and I would have consented to see her only to please the Emperor. It seems, indeed, that she feels more than distant toward me, and I do not understand why: She knows me only through the great sacrifice I made for her. I desire, as she does, the Emperor's happiness, and that sentiment should draw her to me. But none of this will influence my conduct. I have traced a pattern that I must follow: I shall live in retirement, far from everything, but with dignity and demanding nothing but repose. Botany and the arts will occupy me. In the summer I shall visit the spas, and to be nearer you I have just bought a pretty country place on the shores of Lake Geneva. . . . I shall spend this winter at Navarre . . ."

# 3

# *The Châtelaine of Navarre*

JOSEPHINE and her retinue arrived at the château of Navarre on November 22. A thick fog enveloped the great trees of the park and floated over the valley, hiding the rivers and the bay. It was a desolate landscape that made the dilapidated château seem even more melancholy.

The interior had been restored by the architect Berthault, and it was now completely furnished so as to appear habitable —at least more habitable than the little manor house separated from it by a wide courtyard. Around the big drawing room, Berthault had disposed a music room, a billiards room, and a game room. By adding wall partitions he had provided a sufficient number of bedrooms to accommodate the ladies in waiting. On the walls of the Empress's bedroom were hung the historical paintings by Rive that she had sent from Geneva.

To keep the vast rooms warm, a considerable quantity of wood and charcoal had to be burned, and the fireplaces consumed more than "thirty loads" a day. Even so, it was not warm enough in the Empress's rooms and the reception rooms on the ground floor. Everywhere in the château an icy wind blew, often with such force that the window curtains flapped like wings.

A number of pretty girls from poor families became protégées of Josephine at this time. Her cousin, and godchild,

Stéphanie Tascher, who had been married three years before, and unhappily, to the Prince d'Arenberg, sought refuge at the château of Navarre. From Geneva, the Empress had brought a friend of Madame Tallien, a man by the name of Van Berchem who had been ruined by gambling and women. Josephine made him master of the hunt, and the former *bon vivant* with the "build of a Swiss drum major" made himself popular among the ladies.

One hundred and fifty servants, with their wives and children, were employed on the household staff. Parisian tradesmen flocked to Navarre, bringing down the latest novelties. Petitioners for favors at times almost forced the doors of the château, adding to the liveliness of the court. Every morning Josephine dictated letters to Deschamps, her secretary, letters of recommendation to ministers and under-secretaries or to secretaries of the Emperor.

Breakfast was at half-past ten, except on Sundays and holidays when the Empress attended mass, and lasted an hour. The Empress always sat between the two most eminent persons present, and when Queen Hortense came to Navarre, she could also designate the two persons she wished to have seated beside her. The first lady in waiting, Madame d'Arberg, likewise enjoyed this privilege. The abundant courses were served on very beautiful china that was a gift of the Emperor. One footman stood behind each guest, and behind the Empress's chair there were two.

After breakfast, in fine weather, they went out of doors for a stroll in the park. Then the ladies returned to their tapestries and needlework, while one of the chamberlains read aloud to them.

Distinguished people of Evreux were invited to dinner. These included the prefect, the mayor, the judge of the criminal court, and the bishop—Monseigneur Bourlier, a sociable man and a friend of Talleyrand, a gourmet who appreciated the exquisite food served at the Empress's table. In the evening there was music. The Empress played billiards with the master of the hunt or backgammon with the bishop—and was always amazed when she won. Sometimes there was conversation by the fireside, and when the bishop was there the conversation was particularly lively.

It was a monotonous but not unpleasant life, declared Madame de Rémusat in a letter. "Time passes here in a singular way; we are always together, we do not do much, we almost don't talk, and yet we're not bored. The same hours bring the same occupations, and we never know if it is today or tomorrow. . . . We are seven women living here in the greatest friendliness. There is only one of the number who is really pretty, and we let her know it and take pleasure from the fact. We live and let live. I am allowed to be lazy, sometimes absent-minded, and even sad, if it suits me. In short, we are given complete freedom . . ."

Josephine no longer suffered from the migraine that had formerly tormented her. She kept more regular hours, and the anguish over the divorce and the horror of exile had diminished. As a result she put on weight, or, as she put it, became as "plump as a good farmwife from Normandy."

In December she had good news from Eugène: His wife, the Princess Augusta, had given birth to a boy. Josephine wrote at once to her son to congratulate him: "My dear Eugène, you could not give me better news or news more eagerly awaited than this."

Eugène had sent his equerry, Count Caprara, to Paris to inform the Emperor of the birth of the prince, and in her letter Josephine mentioned that she expected Count Caprara to stay a few days at Navarre on his return journey. She had invited him to do so, although the château provided few pleasures. "The life I lead," she wrote, "is the life of a châtelaine. My circle of acquaintances is not very large. I now have with me seven or eight ladies and one or two gentlemen at the most, which gives the château something of the atmosphere of a convent. You can imagine how edified and amused Caprara will be! He will take walks when the weather is fine, and on rainy days he will stay with us in the drawing room where Monsieur de Viel-Castel will read aloud to him."

In her letter to Eugène, Josephine goes into some detail regarding her health: "I was not very well for the first few days here, perhaps because of the humidity. They gave me an emetic which stopped the fever, and I should feel very well at present except for a slight pain in my eyes. My eyes, however, are still good enough to see my grandson if he were here . . ."

Josephine complained to everyone about her eyes. "It comes from having shed too many tears," Hortense said to her one day.

"But since my return to France," she replied, "I only cry now and then."

In this almost unchanging and joyless life, what a pleasure Hortense's arrival was to Josephine! The Empress's entourage greeted her with less pleasure, for since Hortense had lived at the new Imperial court, where she gave drawing lessons to the young Empress Marie Louise, she was used to rigorous etiquette, and deplored the lack of decorum that prevailed at Navarre.

When Eugène came to visit, there was always gaiety. He invited the ladies to go fishing with him, after which they would take their catch to the kitchen to have a meal of fried fish on the spot. Prince Eugène's gentle practical jokes, the frights he gave the young girls on boatrides, the pranks he played on them in the château corridors, and his gifts, all made him adored. Neither the prestige of the Empress nor her repose benefited, however. There was a diminution of respect, a familiarity that abolished the hierarchy of rank. According to Madame d'Arberg, life was "at sixes and sevens."

But pleasure and love flourished. The Comte de Pourtalès

took Madame Gazzani to view the romantic sites, then, after having satisfied the demands of the beautiful *lectrice*, went off to whisper sweet nothings to Louise de Castellane. Madame de Colbert responded to the flirtatious overtures of Monsieur de la Briffe. Even the Princesse d'Arenberg did not shut her ears to propositions made by Monsieur de Guitry. During a journey to Evreux, General Wattier saw Mademoiselle de Mackau, and was at once attracted to her as she was to him. He saw his destiny in her eyes, and Josephine permitted them to marry. There were other romances that ended in marriage, too.

The Empress was indulgent, considering that nothing was more natural than flirtations and love affairs between young men and women, especially young women who were pretty, and men who had no other diversion. But she kept a watchful eye on them all the same, so that there would be no shadow of a scandal at Navarre. She gained the confidence of the young girls she had gathered about her, gave them advice, and married them off after settling dowries on them.

Napoleon did not forget Josephine. Though he wrote her only rarely, his letters were always affectionate, and sometimes teasing. In reply to her New Year's greetings, he wrote: "I thank you for what you tell me. I note with pleasure that you are happy. They say that at Navarre there are more women than men." He approved of the marriages she planned for her protégées: "I see nothing against the marriage of Mademoiselle de Mackau and Wattier; the general is a decent sort. . . . I hope to have a son. I will let you know at once."

Nevertheless, as a result of reports that came to him, the Emperor insisted that ceremony be observed at Navarre as severely as at the Tuileries. When he heard that Josephine permitted her chamberlains to wear ordinary dress when accompanying her on excursions, he wrote to Madame d'Arberg, calling her attention not only to the expenses of the Empress's household, but also referring to matters of decorum: "The Empress Josephine was crowned Empress; that is an unchangeable fact. Consequently, she must always be respected." Thereupon he ordered that she never go out without being accompanied by officers in uniform.

From that day on, the Empress had a guard of twenty-five *cuirassiers*. When she went for a stroll in the forest of Evreux, the guard on duty escorted her. And around her open carriage there were fourteen prancing mounted horse, with an officer and a trumpeter.

Meanwhile, at Evreux and in all the department of Eure, the praises of the good Empress were being sung. Her presence seemed to have brought joy and well-being everywhere. Upon her arrival, Josephine had found swamps infecting the countryside, and at her orders, the land was drained. She gave her patronage to charities, relieved miseries that were pointed out to her, and scattered alms and pensions. For orphans she founded a school where the children were taught to make lace and received a complete education. To the inhabitants of Evreux, she gave a great stretch of land on which she had a theater built. She returned to the town a promenade that had been taken away, after purchasing gardens to enlarge it, planted with ten thousand rose bushes.

At the beginning of March, 1811, the people of Evreux were making great preparations to celebrate, in Josephine's honor, the feast day of Saint Joseph. On the nineteenth, at ten in the morning, a troupe of pretty young girls came to offer Josephine the city's greetings and best wishes. Under a dome of flowers, carried as a dais, the mayor's daughter advanced, holding in her arms a bust of the Empress. In presenting it to her, the little girl recited a greeting in rhyme. Josephine gave her two kisses, as she thanked her. The young visitors stayed for luncheon, and at the moment of departure the Empress gave each of them a present.

Fearing to displease the Empress Marie Louise, and thereby the Emperor, Josephine forbade all public demonstrations— but in vain. All night long fireworks illumined the town and the villages for ten leagues around.

That night, after dinner, the Empress received in the great octagonal drawing room a strange group of peasants, both men and women, dressed in their Sunday best. They were the Empress's court in disguise, come to offer her their greetings on her saint's day. For the occasion they had composed a song, putting new words to an old tune. The verse was sheer doggerel, but touching in its sentiment of devotion and praise for the Empress Josephine, her grandeur and benevolence. It ended with "Long may she live! Long may her glory endure!"

After repeating the *vivas*, the best singers of the troupe were heard one after the other in couplets praising their sovereign— Madame d'Audenarde, Madame Gazzani, Madame de Colbert, Mademoiselle de Mackau, and Mademoiselle de Castellane. Finally, Mademoiselle Georgette Ducrest, who was particularly fond of the Empress, sang in a charming voice, a little shaky with emotion, a couplet to the tune of "Joseph," an old folksong.

Another "peasant" couple came in, announcing themselves as Colette and Mathurin—Madame Octave de Ségur and Monsieur de Viel-Castel in disguise. The couplets they sang recalled the gifts granted by the Empress to Evreux, how she had drained the land, adorned it with trees and roses, established schools, and so on.

At the end of all these performances, Monsieur de Turpin-Crissé presented the Empress with a pack of cards that he had himself designed and painted: The faces on the name cards were portraits of habitués of the château of Navarre.

The festivities continued the next day, and Josephine gave a ball on the night of the twentieth, after a dinner given in her honor by the mayor. She did not attend the dinner in person but sent her ladies in waiting to represent her, and remained alone at the château with Madame d'Arberg.

About eight o'clock all the bells of the town began to ring. Then the roar of a cannon was heard. Josephine and Madame d'Arberg exchanged anxious glances. At that moment the post-office director arrived and handed the Empress an envelope. She opened it, and after glancing over the message, said to her companion, "The King of Rome is born." Then, turning toward the messenger, she added graciously, "The Emperor can have no doubt of the sincerity with which I share in his joy at this event. I am inseparable from his destiny and shall always rejoice in his happiness."

A few hours later Prince Eugène, sent by Napoleon, arrived to give a detailed account of the event. Josephine immediately wrote a letter of congratulation to Napoleon, who replied as follows:

"My dear, I have received your letter and I thank you. My son is big and very healthy. I hope he will have a good life. He has my chest, my mouth, my eyes. I hope he will fulfill his destiny." To reassure Josephine about his intentions in regard to her and Eugène's future, the Emperor added: "I have always been well pleased with Eugène; he has never caused me any sorrow."

Josephine was curious to hear from Eugène how the Bonaparte family had greeted the birth of Napoleon's son and heir. Eugène described their mortification, laughingly imitating the frowns and smirks of Caroline and Pauline, who waited, during the Empress's labor, in an adjacent room. They realized that their credit with their brother would now decline and, unable to hide their chagrin, they were extremely nervous.

Eugène's imitations of their attitudes and agitated gestures made everyone laugh aloud and, infected by the general good humor, Josephine joined in the laughter. Yet the coming of the King of Rome into the world removed her last hope of ever seeing Eugène succeed his adoptive father, Napoleon, on the throne of France.

# 4

## *Josephine's Family Joys and Troubles*

B<sup>Y EARLY AUTUMN</sup>, Josephine was again in ill health, complaining of headaches and a roaring in the ears. She returned to Malmaison, where Dr. Corvisart applied the remedies of the day—cupping and leeches. She had barely recovered from her illness when she received an irritated letter from the Emperor: "Put your affairs in order. Spend no more than 1,500,000 francs, and save as much every year. That will give you a reserve of 15,000,000 in ten years for your grandchildren.... Instead of doing this, I am told that you have debts; that is very bad. Take care of your own affairs; don't give money to everyone who asks.... Consider what a bad opinion I would have of you, if I learned you were in debt with an income of 3,000,000 francs."

Napoleon, at the peak of his career, looked into the future and saw it darkly. He had extended France's power to the Baltic, but war with Russia was threatening. No wonder he was irritated over Josephine's debts, and thinking of the future of her grandchildren.

It was a fact that Josephine's debts had been steadily mounting. Everyone victimized her, including the members of her own household. She began, however, to administer her affairs with greater economy when she learned that Napoleon wanted to cut by a million francs the annual allowance he had drawn from the Crown Treasury for her.

"Holding back a million," she wrote in panic to Eugène, "will make it impossible for me to keep up my present style of living. But the reason for the loss of the money would hurt me much more than the loss of the money itself. You know that money privations are not my worst sufferings."

Malmaison was near enough to Paris so that Josephine could entertain there a great deal—and lavishly. Her Neapolitan cook, Ruccesi, was becoming famous for the dishes he prepared at Malmaison, as were Josephine's hothouses where exotic fruits ripened.

Besides the cost of entertaining, there were the gifts and dowries she bestowed when any of her protégées married. And that year a veritable whirlwind of marriages blew over Malmaison. Madame d'Arberg discovered that Monsieur de Pourtalès was having an affair with Mademoiselle de Castellane: She had caught him slipping a letter under the young lady's door. Josephine, informed of this, had the guilty parties brought to her, took them for a stroll in the park, and reprimanded the girl. Then, to test the seducer, she said to Mademoiselle de Castellane, "You possess nothing but your name. Monsieur de Pourtalès is rich. Surely you can't believe he wants to marry you?"

"I would be only too happy!" exclaimed the gentleman.

The Empress smiled. "Well then, I will give her a hundred thousand francs' dowry and her trousseau."

The marriage took place early in November. Then, on January 22, 1812, another marriage was celebrated—that of Annette de Mackau and General Wattier de Saint-Alphonse—with another demand on Josephine's exchequer. Josephine dowered Mademoiselle Avrillon, one of the wardrobe mistresses, who was the daughter of the mulatto Malvinia and the doorkeeper at Bois-Préau. Josephine had resolved and promised to economize, but dowries, allowances, and trousseaux dissolved her good intentions.

And she could not stop buying. She bought statues, seeds, and shrubs. To anyone who visited her hothouses, she gave beautiful "samples": a purple magnolia tree to Madame de Chateaubriand, to the prefect of Loire-et-Cher some plants from Pennsylvania. Monsieur de Candolle received valuable bulbs, and Baron de Rouvroy some laurel bushes. To her lady visitors she gave shawls. Her generosity knew no bounds.

One day, Monsieur de Pourtalès admired a dress of rare cashmere she was wearing. "Some very fine waistcoats could be made of that," he remarked. Josephine at once went to her rooms, took off the dress, and, wielding the scissors herself, cut it up into pieces, which she distributed among the chamberlains. She paid high prices for Monsieur de Turpin's paintings, and sometimes she would add a diamond of great price in payment.

Not without reason, she was indignant at rumors being circulated by her cousins, the Taschers. According to them, she was ungenerous, and scorned and neglected them. Josephine complained of this in a letter to Eugène, recalling that she had given 60,000 francs to the eldest of the three Tascher sons at his marriage. When the second son had married the niece of Queen Julie of Spain (the wife of Joseph Bonaparte, who was then King Joseph I of Spain) she had given the bride a set of jewels worth 30,000 francs, and only recently had paid off a note of 32,000 francs for him. As for the youngest son, who lived with his sister, Josephine gave him an allowance of 6,000 francs, and paid for lessons that were given to him by her librarian, the Abbé Halna. Her distant relatives were almost as well treated.

"I give an allowance of a thousand écus to Sanois," she wrote Eugène, "12,000 francs to Monsieur Dugué, 3,000 francs to Monsieur de Copons. I pay for the upkeep and education of Monsieur Sainte-Catherine's three children, 1,000 écus allowance to Madame Duplessis, 2,000 francs allowance to Madame Tascher, whose husband is in the army, and another allowance of 1,000 francs to one of the Taschers who is a nun. You see, dear Eugène, that I am not such a bad relative as they would have people believe, and surely I have the right to do what I can for people who are near me and contribute every day to my happiness."

While Josephine threw her money about, the new steward, Monsieur de Montlivault, who had replaced the extravagant Monsieur de Monaco, haggled like a peddler over everything, ingeniously managed to find new resources, had the woods cleared, rented off pieces of land, kitchen gardens, and even the château of Buzenval.

Napoleon came occasionally to Malmaison, and each time Josephine expressed the desire to see the little King of Rome. He held off, for he knew the Empress Marie Louise would never consent to take her son to Malmaison. But finally he arranged it so that Josephine might have her wish. Josephine was notified that Madame de Montesquiou was to take the child to the château of Bagatelle one day, and she was prompt for the rendezvous.

"Dear child," Josephine murmured, as she took the little heir to the throne in her arms, "you will perhaps one day know what you cost me!" Then she covered him with kisses and handed him back to the governess.

When Marie Louise heard of this incident, she was furious. To gain back her good graces, Napoleon had to promise never to return to Malmaison.

But he did come back—on April 30, 1812—to say good-by before setting forth, with the Grand Army, to invade Russia.

There were other sad farewells, for Eugène would go with his stepfather on this campaign. Before taking command of the Fourth Army Corps, he came to kiss his mother good-by. He was leaving his wife, the Princess Augusta, pregnant, and

Josephine promised him she would go to Milan for her daughter-in-law's confinement.

Thus, by mid-July Josephine was in Milan with her daughter-in-law at the Villa Bonaparte, surrounded by her grandchildren. There were three now, for Eugène and Augusta had two daughters and a son, all fine healthy children. Four days after the Empress's arrival, Augusta gave birth to another girl, who was named Amelia. Josephine remained in Milan during the entire month of August, charmingly playing the role of grandmother.

In September, after the victorious Battle of Borodino, in which Prince Eugène and his army corps (an Italian contingent) distinguished themselves, Eugène wrote a letter of thanks to his mother from the battlefield: "I cannot thank you enough for the care and kindness you have given my little family. You are adored in Milan, as everywhere. I have had letters that tell me charming things about you. You have turned the heads of everyone who has met you."

The French armies in Spain had suffered frightful losses, but now, according to rumors that drifted back to Paris from Poland and Russia, the Grand Army was suffering even greater losses. A rumor was even circulated that Napoleon had died in Russia, and the latest bulletins of the army gave no reassurance against the worst disasters.

Josephine went to Aix, and then to Prégny in October. It was there, on the shores of Lake Geneva, that she heard of General Malet's conspiracy to seize power. Malet was captured and shot, but other conspiracies were being woven everywhere—in Naples, Holland, Spain, in France itself. Josephine returned to Paris and Malmaison two days after the execution of General Malet.

The anxious month of November drew to a close, and the first snow of December powdered the roofs of Paris. On De-

cember 19, 1812, Napoleon returned to the Tuileries, bitter
and care-worn, after his epic retreat from Moscow.

Josephine longed to console and cheer him, and she cursed
Marie Louise for preventing their meeting. She had been
categorically forbidden ever to see the little King of Rome
again, but in this time of trouble she thought of another son
of Napoleon, Alexandre, son of Marie Walewska.

Josephine invited the Countess Walewska to bring
her child to Malmaison. Calamity had overtaken Marie
Walewska's native land, Poland, which the Russians had
occupied; she was a refugee in France. All Josephine's jealousy
and wrath had been dispelled. She felt for the unfortunate
countess and her child only a kind of benevolent and affectionate curiosity. When they came to Malmaison, Josephine overwhelmed the child with toys and caresses.

She passionately loved children, enjoying their prattle, and
liked to indulge them. During that melancholy winter when
Malmaison received but few visitors, Hortense's two little sons,
Napoleon and Louis (nicknamed "Oui-Oui"), were almost
her only joy. They became the masters of the place, and their
grandmother, who was so fond of her gardens and hothouses,
even let them cut some of her most exotic flowers, and encouraged them to break off pieces of sugar cane to suck.
Usually she anticipated their desires, but one day she said,
"Tell me what you want me to give you the most." The elder
of the two, Napoleon, said he wanted a watch with a portrait
of his mother in it. Louis, who had never gone out except in
a carriage, asked permission to walk in the mud with the little
street urchins.

Josephine particularly doted on Oui-Oui, who was so pretty
that he was sometimes called "Princess" Louis. She marveled
at his every word and often wrote in minute detail to Hortense,
who was traveling in Switzerland, regarding the boys:

"You cannot imagine how happy you have made me by

leaving them here," she wrote. "They create a feeling of life around me."

And when Hortense feared her mother was being too indulgent, Josephine declared: "Your children are in perfect health, their complexions are pink and white; I assure you they have not had the slightest illness. What you prescribed for their diet and their studies is being followed exactly. When they have worked well during the week I let them lunch and dine with me on Sunday." She described some unusual gifts she had made them: "The day Monsieur de Turpin arrived, I had received from Paris two little golden hens that, by some mechanism, lay silver eggs. I gave them to the children as a present from you . . ."

She always reported to Hortense the amusing things the children said. In one such letter the anecdote concerned Oui-Oui, then not quite five years old:

"I must tell you about a pretty response of little Oui-Oui. He was reading to the Abbé Bertrand a fable on the subject of metamorphosis. When asked to explain the meaning of the word, he said, 'I wish I could change myself into a little bird. I would then fly away at the hour of your lesson; but I would come back when Herr Haze, my German teacher, arrives.' 'Why, Prince,' responded the abbé, 'that is not very kind.' 'Oh,' said Oui-Oui, 'what I said was only about the lesson, not the man.' Don't you agree with me that's a witty retort? It would be impossible to get out of a difficulty with more finesse and grace."

When Hortense came to take her sons away with her to Dieppe, the parting was heart-rending for Josephine. Following their departure, she tried to drive away melancholy by giving a great many dinner parties, but it is doubtful that she succeeded. She knew that the world was seething, and that the fate of the Empire hung in the balance. At a time when Napoleon was daily having to make decisions of world-wide importance, she must have felt more keenly than ever her oblivion.

To cheer herself up, she wrote Eugène that "the best society" came to her dinner parties at Malmaison. Only the Bonapartes seemed to ignore her very existence. For more than two years not one of them had come to visit her.

# 5

## Collapse of an Empire

IN MAY, 1813, Prince Eugène received orders from the Emperor to return to Italy and raise a new army. The Grand Army of the French Empire, the greatest army that had ever been assembled under one flag, had dwindled away to almost nothing in the Russian campaign. The countries Napoleon had bound together were now breaking apart. Frederick William III of Prussia had signed an alliance with the Czar, and there was a great flocking to arms for a "war of liberation," to throw off the French yoke. Everywhere, Napoleon was being betrayed by the very men in whom he had put most trust. The king he had set on the throne of Sweden had signed, in March, a treaty with the arch-enemy, England.

Toward the end of May, Napoleon attacked the Allies at Bautzen and Lutzen, victoriously but with terrible losses, and drove the Allies back to Dresden. In July, the great Congress of Prague was set up, but Metternich and Caulaincourt negotiated in vain and by August the Congress dissolved, having accomplished nothing. Immediately thereafter, Austria declared war upon France.

To take her mind off Napoleon's troubles, Josephine kept herself busy with her art collection and her horticultural interests, her sheepfolds and dairies, and her aviaries at Malmaison. She had brought back from Switzerland a Swiss family to be the skilled overseers of the livestock. New outbuildings were constructed for new dairies, sheepfolds, and aviaries.

In addition to these occupations Josephine entertained a great many important people, for since Napoleon's departure for Germany, and the declaration of war by Empress Marie Louise's father against France, crowds of courtiers and generals flocked to Malmaison. In the gold drawing room, fifty or sixty people were entertained every night.

Before rejoining the army, Marshal Oudinot, who had been made Duc de Reggio two years before, brought his second wife to Malmaison to present her to Josephine. Oudinot had served in the Russian campaign, and it may be imagined that Josephine questioned him closely about events there. She took the duke and duchess for a tour of the gardens and hothouses and cut a spray of camellias for the duchess. The duke complimented her on her apparent good health, and she replied, with a resigned smile, "Yes, it seems to agree with me to be no longer a reigning Empress."

Then, once again, Josephine was left in solitude, as the news of the armies came in, each report adding darkness to the already heavy gloom. After the defeats of Oudinot at Gross-Beeren, Ney at Denewitz, and Macdonald at Katzbach, and after the betrayal of Moreau and Bernadotte and Murat, news came that the Allies had crossed the Elbe. In October, there was Napoleon's terrible defeat at Leipzig, and Josephine's despondency became despair.

Through the King of Bavaria, his father-in-law, Prince Eugène was invited by the Austrians to sign a separate armistice, but Eugène refused to betray his benefactor. The slowness of communications, however, prevented him from following the Emperor's orders exactly, and Napoleon felt himself betrayed by his adopted son just when his help was most needed: The Allies were invading France.

At Napoleon's request, Josephine wrote an urgent letter to Eugène, on February 9, 1814: "Do not lose a moment, dear

Eugène, no matter what the obstacles. Redouble your efforts to fulfill the commands the Emperor gave you. He has just written me on the subject. He intends that you should cross the Alps with reinforcements, leaving in Mantua, and elsewhere in Italy, only Italian troops. His letter ends with these words: 'France above all! France needs all her sons!' So come, dear son, make haste. Never will you have better served the Emperor. I can assure you that every minute is precious. I know your wife has made arrangements to leave Milan. Tell me if I can be of use to her. Adieu, dear Eugène, I have time only to embrace you and to repeat: Come quickly!"

But Prince Eugène, Viceroy of Italy, had his hands full trying to govern a country that was in complete upheaval, and British forces were preparing to land in Leghorn and Genoa. Napoleon's doubt of his loyalty wounded Prince Eugène cruelly, and he earnestly reaffirmed his devotion to his adoptive father. But he remained—to Josephine's despair—in Italy.

Despite the feats accomplished by Napoleon in the field during those tragic days, despite the heroic deeds of the last of the Old Guard and the young "Marie Louise soldiers" of the Grand Army, the Allies were approaching Paris. . . .

At Malmaison, in the evenings, the ladies no longer did tapestry work; instead, they prepared bandages for the ambulance corps. Josephine, working side by side with them, heard all the whispered rumors. Everyone seemed to take it for granted that the Emperor was facing defeat. And alas, Madame de Rémusat, the Viel-Castels, the Turpins, Messieurs Pourtalès, Montlivault, upon whom the Empress Josephine had heaped honors and riches, were conspiring, intriguing, and scheming, without Josephine's knowledge.

Josephine's courtiers, footmen, and husbandmen were all at the front, now. There were only a few wounded men to guard Malmaison. Everyone advised the Empress to leave and find a safer refuge. But where to go?

In her distress, Josephine wrote to Hortense, who was at

Chartres: "I cannot tell you how unhappy I am. I have had courage in unfortunate situations before, and I shall have courage to endure these reverses of fortune. But I do not have the courage to bear the absence of my children, and the uncertainty about their fate."

Her ladies in waiting often heard her exclaim, "How he must be suffering!" And she expressed a longing to be at the Emperor's side in his hour of trial. She was finally persuaded to leave for Navarre, and set out at dawn on March 29, 1814.

Early in April, Hortense joined her mother at the château of Navarre, bringing her two children with her. Together they spent a tense week, avidly questioning everyone arriving from Paris. They learned that the city had capitulated, that the Allies had entered the capital. Josephine went about in a daze, and could be heard muttering meaningless words in reply to remarks that she seemed not to hear or understand.

One night toward the end of April there was the sound of carriage wheels in the driveway, followed by a loud knocking at the door. It was the Baron de Maussion, one of the councilors of state. Josephine flung on a dressing gown to receive him and hear his dreadful news. The Empress Marie Louise, who had been acting as regent, had left Paris with her son to take refuge at Rambouillet, while waiting for her father, the Emperor Francis. She had announced her wish to return to Austria. But this was not the worst: Napoleon, betrayed by Talleyrand, the Senate, and some of his own generals, had abdicated. He was to be sent into exile.

Josephine listened in silence, wild-eyed, as if without understanding. She heard the Baron de Maussion say "exile" and "Elba."

"Come with me. You must tell this to my daughter," she said, and, taking a candlestick, motioned the baron to follow her. They crossed the courtyard toward the apartments occupied by Hortense who, awakened by the noise, was impatiently waiting for the news.

The Baron de Maussion had to tell his story all over again. As he repeated it, Josephine finally understood: The Emperor was vanquished; the Empire was no more; the Bourbons were returning; Napoleon was to be sent away in exile.

With a cry, she threw herself into her daughter's arms.

The last hope of seeing Napoleon again left her. He had abdicated and was leaving for the isle of Elba. She could do nothing to save him. Distraught, she bent all her thoughts upon saving her children.

From Navarre she wrote to Eugène: "... How I have suffered at the way they have treated the Emperor! What dastardly things they print in the newspapers, and what ingratitude on the part of those he showered with honors! But there is now nothing to hope for, all is finished. He has abdicated.... Anything you might do for his cause would be useless. Act now for your family. Your sister and her children are with me. Her destiny and mine have not as yet been decided. But you, dear son, where are you? What are you doing? How is Augusta?... I long to have news of you and yours. I live in a state of terrible anxiety."

# 6

## The Death of Josephine

ON MAY 5, King Louis XVIII entered Paris.

The Empress Josephine's "court," which had already dwindled, began to disintegrate, until there remained only a few ladies in waiting and the most faithful chamberlains. Most of the ladies and gentlemen in waiting were from old titled families, and they felt their ancient and true allegiance to the Bourbons. Madame de Rémusat and Madame d'Audenarde had been among the first to transfer their allegiance to the King and the Allies. Messieurs de Pourtalès, de Turpin, de Viel-Castel, and Montlivault soon followed their example.

The Allied sovereigns seemed to be resolved to protect the Empress Josephine, Hortense, and Prince Eugène. Monsieur de Nesselrode, the minister of Czar Alexander of Russia, came to Navarre to ask Josephine to return to Malmaison; and the Prince of Saxe-Coburg informed her that the Czar wished to make the acquaintance of the Empress and her daughter Hortense. Josephine, finding herself without protection, could not refuse to accept these overtures. But Hortense refused to follow her, saying that her loyalties remained with the Empress Marie Louise, who had taken refuge at Rambouillet.

Hortense was coldly received by Marie Louise, who told her, not without embarrassment, that she expected her father, the Emperor of Austria, on the morrow, and that in any case she would prefer to be alone.

"He does not know you," she added, "and I fear he would be ill at ease in your presence."

The Empress Marie Louise seemed to dread her father's impending visit. When Hortense tried to reassure her, she learned why. "Oh, my dear Hortense," Marie Louise said, "do you think my father will compel me to follow Napoleon to the isle of Elba?"

Amazed and disgusted, Hortense did not reply. So that explained her troubled behavior! Remembering her mother who, in the midst of misfortunes, had never forgotten the man she had always loved, Hortense left Rambouillet and returned to Malmaison, where Josephine was again in residence.

When Hortense arrived, the courtyard was full of Cossacks, and she was told that the Empress Josephine was strolling in the garden with the Czar of Russia. She found them near the hothouse, where Josephine kissed her and presented her to the Czar: "This is my daughter," she said. "I commend her and my grandchildren to Your Majesty's kindness."

The Czar offered his arm to Hortense who replied, in a constrained way, to his questions. Josephine left, to rejoin them shortly afterward in the château, where she at once noticed Hortense's cool attitude. With a sincerity that could not be doubted, Alexander deplored the rigors of war and, caressing Hortense's two little sons, asked her, "What do you want me to do for them?"

Cool and dignified, Hortense replied that she asked nothing for her children, although she appreciated the interest His Majesty showed in them. The Czar withdrew, charmed by Josephine, but slightly offended by Hortense.

When he had gone, Josephine reprimanded Hortense, who defended herself by saying she found it impossible to show cordiality to a man who was the declared personal enemy of the Emperor Napoleon.

Nonetheless, it was thanks to the Czar that Hortense was authorized to keep her children, and given an allowance of 400,000 francs. And he arranged that the Empress Josephine should retain an income of a million. To Prince Eugène, former Viceroy of Italy, a comfortable estate near Munich was eventually given, and he was made Duke of Leuchtenberg and Prince of Eichstätt. Finally, despite the opposition of the other Allied powers, Alexander secured for Napoleon the sovereignty of the isle of Elba.

When the Czar returned to Malmaison, Hortense greeted him with less coldness. He took her children on his knees, caressing them even more tenderly than the first time, and displayed so much deference to both Josephine and Hortense that "he seemed to be asking their pardon for having become necessary to them," as Hortense wrote later.

Apparently Alexander liked the atmosphere of Malmaison, for he returned many times, each time for a longer visit. In the course of these interviews, when the talk turned upon Napoleon, Josephine never denied the affection she still had for the Emperor.

The King of Prussia also asked the honor of paying a visit to the Empress Josephine. And when it became known that these two rulers had visited Malmaison, the other princes felt obliged to put in an appearance. Soon, all the society that had deserted Josephine was flocking back.

Madame de Rémusat presented herself one morning at Malmaison with the avowed object of giving advice. According to her, Josephine must show "a mark of deference for the family that has been called upon to reign." The King's brother, the Comte d'Artois, who had for years been living in exile as the recognized head of the royalist movement, was now in Paris, the center of society. Madame de Rémusat felt that if Josephine hoped to remain in France unmolested, she must "show her adherence to the Bourbons." The scheming woman, with Talleyrand's assistance, had prepared a letter for Josephine to sign, in which she was made to say that she knew not what her status had been or was now, and implored the King to decide upon it. Josephine refused to sign and told Madame de Rémusat she would think it over.

She was so troubled by this obvious perfidy that she decided to tell the Czar about the odious letter and ask his advice. The Czar indignantly assured her that no one would trouble her and that she could always count on his coming to her defense. The Empress, reassured, wrote a curt note of refusal to her former lady in waiting to end the chapter.

Eugène arrived in Paris a few days after Louis XVIII had taken up his residence at the Tuileries, and it was then, after meeting the Czar, that he was given his titles and estate in Germany.

The Czar had to overcome the unfriendly attitude of the King's minister, the Duc de Blacas, to carry out the arrangements he made in favor of the Empress Josephine and Hortense. These arrangements provided that Josephine was to keep Malmaison and Navarre; Hortense, her château at Saint-Leu, now a duchy.

Satisfied at having assured their future, the Czar expressed his wish to see Saint-Leu, and on the fourteenth of May he lunched at the château with Josephine and Hortense. No one else was present except Marshal Ney, who was then adroitly posing as a supporter of the Bourbons, and his wife.

During a short carriage ride after this luncheon Josephine caught a chill. She drank a hot herb tea made of lime blossoms and orange flowers, and lay down for a while. For the sake of her important guests, who had remained on for dinner, she got up to preside at the table. But she could not eat, and retired early to bed.

The next day, she felt well enough to return to Malmaison, and to receive a number of people that night. She managed to be her usual cordial and smiling self, addressing kindly remarks to everyone except Madame de Staël, who had come to look at the Empress, of whom she had been so envious, in her misfortune. Josephine was very curt with her.

After her departure, the Empress sat down beside the fire and said to the Duchesse de Reggio, "I have just had a most painful conversation." She paused, looking very agitated and upset. "Would you believe it?" she went on. "Among other questions, Madame de Staël asked me whether I still love the Emperor! She wanted to know what my state of mind was in this present, great misfortune. Could I possibly feel colder toward him today, I, who never ceased loving the Emperor in his happiness?"

Josephine had saved many people from the guillotine in her time. Only a few remembered this, and she suffered from the ingratitude of the others. The Marquis de Rivière, whose life she had saved, came to Malmaison that year to pay his respects. The Marquis de Polignac, who had been implicated in the Cadoudal-Pichegru plot against the Emperor's life in 1804, owed his life to her; she had successfully gained for him the Emperor's mercy; but he was not among those who visited the Empress Josephine in her misfortune.

On May 23, the Grand Duke Constantine and the King of Prussia with his family came to spend the day at Malmaison. Josephine was ill, but she came downstairs to receive them and to stroll in the park with them. It was on this occasion that she caught another cold.

Suffering from chills, nausea, and fever, she was obliged to let Hortense preside at dinner, and the next day she remained in bed. It was in this weakened condition that a newspaper fell into her hands, containing some spiteful references to Napoleon Charles, Hortense's eldest son who had died in Holland and had been interred at Notre Dame. Hortense's reader, Mademoiselle Cochelet, found the Empress weeping.

"Has my daughter read this paper?" Josephine asked, pointing to the item that had disturbed her. "Try to keep her from seeing it."

The paper announced that the dead child's remains were to be removed from the cathedral and buried in a Parisian cemetery.

"Is it possible?" exclaimed Josephine. "They dare to disturb the tombs of the dead! It's like revolutionary times!"

When Hortense reached her side, Josephine was still agitated over the newspaper article. She was coughing, and breathing with difficulty. Dr. Horeau prescribed blood-letting, but the next day her condition became worse, and her pulse was very faint.

That night the Czar was to dine at Malmaison and Josephine wanted to get out of bed, dress, and go downstairs. The physician categorically forbade it. Hortense noticed his worried expression and questioned him anxiously. He did not hide his fears: Josephine's condition was very serious. Frightened, Hortense summoned other physicians: Bourdois, Lamoureux, and Lasserre. Prince Eugène was so upset that he, too, fell ill, and was obliged to remain in bed.

There was no time to forewarn the Czar, and when he arrived, Hortense had him shown up to Eugène's room, where she left the gentlemen to return to her mother. The Czar, she told her, had sent word that he could not dine with them that night, but would dine with them again very soon.

Josephine was very upset at this information. "I'm sure," she said, "that he stayed away tonight because he is embarrassed at having nothing new to tell us about your brother." After a silence, she went on. "We must dare to talk to the Czar about Eugène, since he is the only one who is kindly disposed to us."

Hortense promised to do so, and then brought in her children to bid their grandmother good night. Josephine at once sent them away. "The air is not good here," she murmured. "It might be bad for them." Then she urged her daughter to take some rest; a chambermaid, alone, could sit up with her.

Toward the middle of the night, Josephine several times uttered some rambling remarks about "Bonaparte ... the isle of Elba ... the King of Rome. ..." For a while nothing could be heard but her labored breathing, and she sank into a deep slumber.

Early the next morning, Eugène and Hortense went to her bedroom. She woke up, held out her arms to them, and murmured some unintelligible words. Hortense burst into tears, and was led from the room. The Abbé Bertrand leaned over Josephine to administer the last rites.

A few moments later, Eugène went to his sister's room and threw himself into her arms, weeping and saying, "All is over!"

The Empress Josephine had died one month and ten days after the Emperor's abdication.

# 7

## *"She Was Woman . . ."*

Lᴇss ᴛʜᴀɴ ᴀ ʏᴇᴀʀ after Josephine's death news reached France
that Napoleon had escaped from the isle of Elba and
was on his way to Paris. His old followers rushed to welcome
him, the royalists fled, and on March 20, 1815, Napoleon was
re-acclaimed Emperor of the French at the Tuileries.

Almost immediately he summoned Dr. Corvisart to him.
"So you let my poor Josephine die?" he said.

Dr. Corvisart defended himself by saying he had been ill
at the time, and another physician, a Dr. Horeau, had attended the Empress.

Napoleon immediately called for Dr. Horeau. "You did not
leave the Empress during her entire illness?"

"No, Sire."

"What, according to you, caused the illness?"

"Anxiety . . . grief . . ."

"You believe that?"

Napoleon musingly continued to question Horeau on the
duration of the illness, the remedies employed, and asked
him about the Empress's courage at the moment of death.
Then he fell silent.

"You say she suffered from grief?" he asked suddenly.
"What was the cause of her grief?"

"What had happened, Sire. The position of Your Majesty."

"Ah! Did she speak of me?"

"Often, very often."

"Oh, the good woman! Good Josephine! She truly loved me then?"

"Oh, yes, Sire. . . . One day she told me that had she been Empress of the French, she would have crossed Paris in a carriage and eight, with her household in dress livery, to rejoin you at Fontainebleau and never leave you."

"And she would have done it, sir. She was capable of doing it."

The fitful glory of the Hundred Days followed, ending with Napoleon's final defeat at Waterloo.

While waiting for his fate to be determined, Napoleon visited Malmaison, where Hortense welcomed him.

One day she found him meditating in the garden, and he motioned her to sit beside him on a bench.

"Poor Josephine!" he said. "I cannot get used to this place without her. I can still see her coming down a path to pick those flowers she loved so much . . ."

Then, seeing the grief his words gave Hortense, he added gently and slowly, "We never quarreled except over one subject—her debts. And I scolded her enough about them. I never saw anyone so filled with grace. She was woman in the fullest sense of the word: mercurial, vivacious, and with the kindest of hearts. . . . I want another portrait of her made for me. I would like it to be in a medallion."